THE ROAD NOT TAKEN

THE FASCINATING LIFE OF AN INTERNATIONAL JOURNALIST

DAVID WOODS

WHAT THEY'RE SAYING...

"David Woods conveys humor and insight into the craft of writing."

– THE LANCET

"{Woods's} contributions are straightforward sensible lessons on writing. His incisive observations on the use of 'we' as in 'How are we today?' should embarrass us all."

– BRITISH MEDICAL JOURNAL

"Your book *Paging Doctors* is a delight, one I will keep handy. Your short essays are meaty, full of good sense and good humor, and brilliantly written. It pleases me more than I can say."

– NORMAN COUSINS

Author of Anatomy of an Illness and longtime editor of Saturday Review

"May I thank you most warmly for your presentation of the interview held in Kitty's and my cottage. I'm used over the years to being distorted and abused; you've stuck steadily to what I said in answer to your questions, and I'm duly grateful."

– MALCOLM MUGGERIDGE

The late author, journalist, polemicist, and TV personality

"I enjoyed seeing your journal, and I appreciate very much your patience and industry in touching on so many points involving me and National Review."

– WILLIAM F. BUCKLEY, JR.

American writer and founder of National Review

"He's, like, cool."

– AMANDA
Stepdaughter

THE ROAD NOT TAKEN

THE FASCINATING LIFE OF AN
INTERNATIONAL JOURNALIST

DAVID WOODS

Cover image: Freepik

Cover design and interior formatting provided by Casselberry Creative Design.

Story Sanctum Publishing.
First Edition.

ISBN: 9798864394809

To my darling wife, Shelly Wolf

TABLE OF CONTENTS

FOREWORD

IN HIS WONDERFUL POEM "The Road Not Taken," Robert Frost describes what happens when one finds difficulties in life and career, and is confronted with the need to make the right decision at the right time, often without full knowledge of the possible outcomes. The main theme of the poem is the dilemma that people face when making such decisions.

And so, I embark upon a memoir, retrospections of an octogenarian journalist and editor that could inevitably turn out to be what such eminent scribes as Malcolm Muggeridge (arguably among the most fêted English language writers of the 20th century) called *Chronicles of Wasted Time*, what novelist Graham Greene called *A Sort of Life*, or as the prolific biographer A.N. Wilson titled his own memoir, *A Life of Failed Promises*.

But what follows is my attempt at chronicling my journey. Evelyn Waugh went even further, suggesting "only when one has lost all curiosity about the future has one reached the age to write an autobiography." As I look back on my life, it was as unexpected as it was extraordinary. Never could I have predicted ending up where I did considering where I began.

The First Time I Made Headlines

From its founding in 1785 until almost 200 years later, the august *Times of London* published no news on its front page lest its British upper- and middle-class readers might become agitated or dyspeptic over their breakfast. Instead, in the ubiquitous Times Roman typeface which it invented, the paper carried several columns of births, deaths, personal ads, announcements, business offers, and educational services.

In the issue of Wednesday, March 29, 1939 (No 48,266) there appeared, under Births, the following:

> *"On March 25, 1939, at Benslow Nursing Home, Hitchin {Hertfordshire}, to Cynthia, wife of Squadron Leader W.D. Woods, R.A.F.* [Royal Air Force] *- a son."*

The announcement of my arrival in this world was certainly of little significance except possibly to my parents ... and certainly, compared with some of the other messages on the page, was bland stuff. Consider, for example, this one:

"M.J.- Disappointed over your indifference: shall hope you will not regret it later: nevertheless, it would be comforting to hear. - Sandy."

Or this:

"Rolls Royce Phantom II, late 1935; mileage 19,000... price 1,200 Pounds {about $2,000}."

And this, with Britain heading to war with Germany less than six months later:

"Make your home away from war scares in beautiful health resort..." And: *"Work can be commenced immediately on pillbox, dual purpose air raid shelters..."*

Or the pathetic:

"Man, misfit, alone, been through a bad time, seeks modest job with sincere and understanding folk in remote part of the country."

Perhaps he would have benefited from:

"Be fit, keep fit, Dr Lockwood's system of colon irrigation will clear the poisons. Life then becomes easy."

And housing—how about:

"Cotswolds. - period house for sale ... 3 reception, 6 bedrooms, 7 acres, superb setting, secluded, 4,500 pounds {about $8,000}."

Anyway, very soon after being surrounded by all this, I was whisked away to Wales.

1

A CHILDHOOD IN WALES:
MY EARLIEST MEMORIES

"Years and years and years ago, when I was a boy, when there were wolves in Wales, and birds the colour of red-flannel petticoats whisked past the harp-shaped hills ... when we rode the daft and happy hills bareback, it snowed and it snowed."
–Dylan Thomas, A Child's Christmas in Wales

MY EARLIEST MEMORY is of the small North Wales coastal town of Penmaenmawr, which is Welsh for the less agreeable translation "Big Rock Head." My grandmother, Elisabeth Whiting, had a large Victorian house overlooking the main Wales to London railway line and, beyond it, a mile or so of concrete promenade fronted by a sandy beach and the Irish Sea.

From her house one could see tiny Puffin Island. Shaped

rather like a computer mouse, the island is a bird sanctuary that was once known as Priestholm and was said to have been inhabited by a Saint Seiriol in the 6th century. Beyond it lies the tip of the Druidical island of Anglesey, and on a very clear day one could see the coast of Ireland, but I don't believe I ever did. Much is conjectured in Wales, including the existence of witches and fairies—which is part of its charm.

Mother and son, circa 1940

My mother, Cynthia, was born in Litchfield, Staffordshire, famous for its beautiful three-spired, 13th century cathedral and as the birthplace of one of my heroes, Samuel Johnson, as well as Joseph Addison, who raised the English essay to a degree of perfection never achieved and perhaps never since surpassed, and David Garrick, the foremost actor of the day. Johnson had his early education at Litchfield's 15th century grammar school. My mother, perhaps through some residual spirit in the Litchfield air, took on a lifelong sensibility both for language and for theatrics.

So far as language is concerned, my mother, having been at a so-called finishing school in the South of France, spoke impeccable French. As for theatrics, she did have a love of the stage and even assumed, in an amateur production, a leading role in the Terrence Rattigan play titled "French Without Tears."

Along with her brothers Charles, Glyn, and Sidney, and sisters Alison, Ada, and Betty, she soon made Wales their home. Charles, a colonel in the Royal Welch Fusiliers, an illustrious regiment formed in 1689, lived in an imposing house, Bron Wendon, overlooking the sea at Penmaenmawr, and which is now a retirement home. Glyn, also an army officer, lived farther up the coast at Bangor; and Sidney, a happy-go-lucky jack of all trades, lived even farther afield near the county town of Caernarvon, in a modest house on the estate of Lord Newborough, with Aunt Ada living close by. Alison's Penmaenmawr house, Plas Tirion, was smaller than Charles's, but she and her autodidact husband Edgar were thought to be the moneyed ones of the family ... although there was, strictly speaking, no overt evidence of this.

As in most families, there were skeletons. Little was known or discussed about my mother's father, for instance, although he was reputed to have been some kind of gentleman farmer and veterinarian. And there were other siblings not spoken about, and a shadowy Uncle Herbert who seemed to have had a little-discussed role. Uncle Edgar was much more visible. A Liverpool lad who had left school at 14, he rose to become managing director of an advertising company, and was a man-about-town, sporting impeccable hand-made suits and shoes, and even an opera cloak. He was fond of cars, classical music and good talk, and he had an eye for a pretty woman well into his eighties. Above all, he was a fount of original ideas: as I walked with him along the seashore he would stop a painter or other tradesman, saying, "Excuse me, but have you considered doing it this way?" This was not always well received, but it taught me the value of questioning conventional wisdom.

It was wartime when my mother brought me to Penmaenmawr, which incidentally she always referred to as Pen. She had married a Canadian officer in the Royal Air Force, William Daniel (Bill) Woods, in 1937, and gone with him to service on military bases in Nottingham, Scotland, and Hertfordshire where I was born. The flames of my mother's attraction to Bill were no doubt fanned by his regularly flying a small plane low over her house to woo her. Bill was taken prisoner by the Japanese when Singapore fell in 1942 and spent the rest of the war as a prisoner in Java until he was liberated by American forces in 1945.

Even though the Luftwaffe was pounding and pulverizing London, Liverpool, Exeter, and other British cities, the war hardly seemed to touch North Wales. There was rationing, of course, and the blackout, and my grandmother was forced to give over two floors of her house to families who had been displaced by the bombing. And there was government-issued concentrated orange juice, and packages of dried egg sent from the US—what today we would call care packages.

Ensconced on the top floor of my grandmother's Victorian house was a refugee from what was then Czechoslovakia. He was a talented artist and in fact produced charming watercolors of me and my mother. Erwin Wiesner was a wartime refugee who had somehow hitched a ride on a ship and eventually fled to Poland from where he sailed to Britain. He had practically no command of the English language and I remember once asking him if he would like to have a snack. He proudly drew a picture of a snake all the while making snake-like gestures with his arms. I was intrigued in part because I had never seen a snake and certainly because to give a stranger a snack was charity indeed.

But despite the bleakness of those times and the uncertainty of my father's exact whereabouts or fate, there was a quality of exuberance in the air. To begin with, Penmaenmawr was a holiday resort, and even with the constraints and exigencies of war, it was a place to which vacationers came to bathe in the capricious sea, to walk the sandy beaches, or to climb the mountain on whose lower reaches the town is perched.

Penmaenmawr's population is about 5,000; its principal means of support was tourism and the quarrying of granite that was trundled down the mountain in tiny, noisy trains to the pier where steamers transported it off to various foreign parts. In fact, the tourists who used to flock there in the thousands mainly from the industrial cities of Lancashire have now also discovered foreign parts, tending to prefer in recent years the blandishments of the Costa del Sol or Tuscany.

Pen boasted 20 or more places of worship, and its

claim to fame was that William Ewart Gladstone, four times prime minister of Britain, came there for regular therapeutic bathing exercises, and because, as recorded by Roy Jenkins in his biography *Gladstone,* "he liked the dramatic scenery and found Penmaenmawr a good base for excursions into the misty mountains." He made his first visit there in 1855 and returned almost yearly, "with a fine indifference to the North Wales weather," Jenkins notes. The prime minister continued to brave the local waters well into October, with 27 bathes recorded during his 1861 visit. Gladstone's statue graces Penmaenmawr's main square.

My grandmother was a tiny and fiercely independent woman who smoked prodigiously despite the proscriptions of her daughters. She lived almost her entire 88 years in Wales, yet steadfastly refused to acknowledge that she was situated in a country not her own. In fact, she made a point of over-anglicizing Welsh names, calling, for instance, the nearby village of Dwygyfylchi "Duke of Ulkey." But she was a kindly and generous soul, taking me by bus to the seemingly exotic resort of Llandudno, some 20 miles away, and acceding to my request to go again and again on the open-sided buses that wheezed their way up the winding road to a promontory called the Great Orme, from which there were stunning views of the sea and the coastline.

Llandudno boasts a beautiful semicircular front of elegant, pastel-colored hotels, a pier on which stands a variety theatre, and a statue of Alice Liddell, the young girl on whom Lewis Carroll modeled *Alice in Wonderland.* My favorite were the trams that ran along the main street and even across fields to the adjoining resort town of Colwyn Bay. Some were double deckers with open tops, and one, called the "toast rack," was a flat affair with rows of wooden seats and only a little cabin at each end for a driver.

Llandudno

By an odd twist of fate, I was invited in 2015 to join a committee to help celebrate the 150th anniversary of the first printing of *Alice in Wonderland.* This was a joint venture of the Free Library of Philadelphia and the Rosenbach Museum which is a repository of original manuscripts and letters of such authors as James Joyce, William Blake, and of course, Lewis Carroll.

Three more or less parallel roads run through Pen. The highest, built by the Romans, is a narrow and precipitous route that snakes around the mountainside with a sheer drop to one side. Samuel Johnson, traveling in Wales for the first time in 1774, described the road as hideous. The middle one, taken by the less vertiginous, follows the coastline a little way inland and carried most of the traffic until a gruesome, wide expressway was added in the 1980s that traces the coastline while desecrating its beauty.

It's a good thing that Johnson was not around to see it; he would have been appalled. He did say, though, that "Wales, so far as I have seen of it, is a very beautiful and rich country." He later added: "I have been in five of the six counties of North Wales; and have seen St Asaph and Bangor, the two seats of their bishops; (and) have been upon Penmaenmaur (sic)."

At my grandmother's house, there wasn't much to do; certainly, the privations of wartime meant little in the way of fancy toys or colorful excursions. Although I never felt deprived, I was left pretty much to my own devices, which meant for me, attempting to dig to Australia from her garden and watching the trains go by at the back of the house and the cars, buses and trucks at the front of it. I never actually reached Australia either then or later, but I did develop a lifelong interest in modes of transportation. Moreover, since my mother had, either from over protectiveness or xenophobia, forbidden me to mingle with the local Welsh children, I led a solitary existence, at least so far as people of my own age were concerned.

In her delightful book *A Welsh Childhood*, Alice Thomas Ellis notes that close to where she lived in Pen "there was a little English boy whose name I never knew, who didn't even attempt to fraternize with the natives but played trains all by himself, going choo choo and working his arms like pistons. The local Welsh boys jeered at him in the playground and he once made a response so dignified and so touching that I wept. I can't remember what it was ... but I daresay today I should want to smack him."

I can't swear that that little boy was me; if it was, the description might account for a certain elitism—but I hope not snobbery—that has afflicted me ever since. In fact, in a much later incarnation, I was accused of having been born in a three-piece suit.

That was also when my family's annual pilgrimages to Pen began. Frolicking in the sea, building castles in the sand, and being joined by my brother Richard who was born in 1947 and my sister Liz who came along in 1953. My brother, who is eight years younger than I, was for many years a teacher of Latin and Greek; he now lives on the Greek island of Corfu. For many years he has run a business that involves bringing American middle school kids to Britain in the summer, and he recently founded the Corfu Arts Centre.

My brother Richard

My sister Liz

My sister, 14 years younger than I, lives in London and is a talented artist and medical journalist writing for such periodicals as the *New Scientist, The Daily Mail,* and *The Guardian.*

There was a great to-do in 1950 when the express train, the Irish Mail, traveling at 70 miles an hour from the Welsh port of Holyhead on its way to London, collided with a locomotive that had been left in its path right in front of my grandmother's house. It was August and we were, as usual, on vacation there. The crash occurred at 3:00 a.m. and at daylight I remember seeing the coaches strewn over the tracks. Six people died in the crash and several more were injured. Many local people came to the scene with blankets and sheets, and my uncle Edgar, then aged well over 70, raced to the scene with an axe. Incredibly, I was able to clamber over the precarious wreckage later that day without being accosted and I can recall seeing the blood stains, the shattered glass, and hearing the steam still hissing from the mangled locomotive.

Aftermath of Penmaenmawr train crash, 27 August, 1950 (Source: Wikimedia Commons)

Speaking of Wales

The Welsh language is distinctive. An estimated half million or so of the three million population claim to speak it, and they are mainly in the northwest of the principality. Its origins are Brythonic or Celtic, but it bears little or no resemblance to either the Gaelic of Ireland and Scotland, or to the English connection to Breton and to Cornish. There are words that have a vaguely French intonation, such as *eglws* for church, *ffenester* for window, and *llyrr* for book. "Now I perceive the devil understands Welsh," wrote Shakespeare, and look no further than *Cymreigyddion*, a nationalist cultural organization, or the 58-letter name of a small (!) town in Anglesey that graces the length of the local railway station. Don't try to say it, though: suffice to give it a rough translation, especially after a mouthful of Welsh rarebit—*St. Mary's Church in the hollow of white hazel near a rapid whirlpool and the church of St. Tysilio near the red cave.*

The 58-letter name of a town in Wales (Source: Wikimedia Commons)

Roman influence can be seen in the 13th century Turkish-style castle in Carnarvon where the eldest sons of the reigning English monarch are traditionally crowned Prince of Wales. Wales was subdued and controlled by Edward I in 1280. He built four other major castles at Conwy, Harlech, Criccieth, and Beaumaris on the formerly Druidical Island of Anglesey. The Welsh briefly revolted in 1294, and Edward led an army of 35,000 to quell them again.

The Welsh are noted for their enormous love of rugby and beer and singing, for their relative classlessness, and an egalitarianism that has produced notable leftish politicians such as David Lloyd George, who was Britain's prime minister during World War I, and Aneurin Bevan, the founder of the National Health Service. They are also known for their poets such as Dylan Thomas, artists such as Augustus John, and actors such as Richard Burton, Anthony Hopkins, and Emlyn Williams. Among other notables are Jan Morris, the formerly male auto racing driver who became a woman based upon her surgery in the Middle East, and who has lived for some decades with her wife in a picturesque cottage in North Wales.

Another notable is, of course, Tony Armstrong Jones who shortly after his marriage to Princess Margaret assumed the title of Lord Snowdon, perhaps in recognition of the principality's highest mountain whose pinnacle can be reached by an ancient steam train. In much the same vicinity as Snowdon is the Italianate tourist attraction of Port Marion, a rebuilt village based upon Portofino in Italy.

Wales also has an amazing diaspora. According to John Davies in his *History of Wales,* the Welsh played a significant part in the development of Pennsylvania and it was claimed that a number of the signatories of the Declaration of Independence were of Welsh descent. They had retained a loyalty to the culture of their ancestors, and the publication of Welsh books began in Philadelphia in 1721. A St. David's Society (named for the patron saint of Wales) was established in the city in 1729. The Welsh influence is reflected in some of the place names around Philadelphia: Bala Cynwyd, Narberth, Merion, Llanfair, Gwynedd and Bryn Mawr, for example.

They almost established a separate state in Patagonia (*Y Wladfa Cymrieg*—the Welsh colony) when 20,000 of them settled in that part of the world. But the Argentine government, fearful that the Welsh would seize Patagonia, backed away from granting the colony statehood.

In 1999, Wales achieved a measure of independence when the government of Prime Minister Tony Blair sought devolution of power to that country and to Scotland. The capital city, Cardiff, is now the home of a Welsh Assembly.

While I can claim not a single drop of Welsh blood, my Penmaenmawr kin gave me the moniker *Dafydd ap Gwylym*, the name of the country's first poet, and meaning David, son of William.

My love of Wales is manifested by the fact that I proposed to my American wife, Shelly, in the castle at Conwy, which was built in 1272. My father and mother were married in the same town almost 700 years later, in 1937. And my son Andrew married a Welsh woman, Sarah Evans, his first wife, —in Wales—who gave birth to a daughter, Cerys, whose name derives from the Welsh for "loved one."

Conway Castle, built in 1272, where I proposed to Shelly in 1988

My love of Wales is manifested by the fact that I proposed to my American wife, Shelly, in the castle at Conwy, which was built in 1272. My father and mother were married in the same town almost 700 years later, in 1937. And my son Andrew married a Welsh woman, Sarah Evans, his first wife, —in Wales—who gave birth to a daughter, Cerys, whose name derives from the Welsh for "loved one."

So, there's Welsh blood in the Woods family after all. My granddaughter Cerys is 19, and recently entered medical school at Cardiff University. She is an avid student of both British and American politics and has strong opinions on both which she shares with me on our weekly FaceTime call.

Cerys

2

POSTWAR LONDON:
MY FATHER RETURNS

"We must all turn our backs upon the horrors of the past.
We must look to the future."
–Winston Churchill, speech, 19 September 1946

MY FATHER HAD BEEN CAPTURED in Singapore in 1942 and spent the following three and half years in a Japanese prison camp in Java. Liberated by American forces in 1945, he chose to return to Britain by ship rather than by air, because many allied prisoners upon their release succumbed to sometimes fatal shock when confined in the cramped and noisy aircraft sent to bring them home.

My father came from Halifax, Nova Scotia. He graduated in 1931 from Nova Scotia Technical College, and in 1934 gained a doctorate in engineering from Dalhousie

University in Halifax. He rarely spoke about his experience as a prisoner of war, but my sister Liz, a journalist who then wrote for *The Guardian* and some of the Murdoch papers, wrote a riveting and haunting article. She wrote:

"My mother told me that because Dad had been a prisoner in Java his skin had burned very badly, and doctors were going to make it better. Through my childish eyes he seemed like a monster with a patchwork face. Even though extensive plastic surgery was in its infancy in those days, my dad was privileged to be treated by the eminent reconstructive surgeon Sir Archibald McIndoe who did a fair job in reassembling some of my father's facial features.

"I got used to living in a house with no noise, no shouting or playing boisterous children's games. Our house was deathly quiet, and the family got used to treading on eggshells. For four long years my mother had lived alone in Wales struggling to bring up her small son single handed with just four pounds a month to live on. Dad had spent eight years suppressing any feelings he might have been able to share had he received the therapeutic help he clearly needed. I remember my mother breaking down one day crying with the strain of it all and turned her tear-stained face to Dad. His response was simply: 'I wish I could relieve my feelings so easily.'

"When the Americans finally liberated the camps in August 1945 they were greeted by a shocking sight.

Skeletal figures with swollen bellies and sunken eyes betraying the untold suffering they had endured, shuffled towards them with emaciated, outstretched arms.

"My mother never gave up her faith that my father would one day return home. She had no idea that my father had returned from his experience a broken man. He weighed just 84 pounds when he finally returned to England and mum walked past him twice on the railway station platform before recognizing her beloved husband."

When my father returned to England, our reunion took place in a hotel in the English Lake District where my father had thoughtfully placed his Royal Air Force cap at the end of my bed. Aside from having developed a close relationship with my three uncles, this was the first time that I had encountered an actual father figure. Of course, I was ecstatic to find this new paternal friend and relative.

My father as a 30-year old Flying Officer in the RAF

Like many wives of returning Japanese prisoners of war, my mother realized that life would never be the same again. When the war ended, even though their spirits had been crushed mercilessly, the men who had been through unimaginable suffering were told never to speak of it again, and to "get on with their lives." Yet many like my father found it impossible. He might have recovered physically, but mentally he was fragile. Wracked with guilt over the men who died on his watch, and tortured by nightmares of the horrors he had witnessed, he became prone to dark moods and long bouts of depression.

In rooting through some boxes of old letters my sister came across one from my father to my mother dated October 10, 1942, from Kuala Lumpur in Malaysia, and preceding his capture by only a matter of weeks.

En route from Montréal to Los Angeles, my father wrote, "I met one chap on the train who was unstinting in his praise of the British people generally and the RAF in particular."

He sailed across the Pacific in a Dutch ship, stopping at Honolulu on the way. At Surabaya in the Dutch East Indies, he haggled with native shopkeepers about prices of beautiful woodcarvings. He continued, "Had I been going back the other way, how I shall look forward to it—I would've bought a couple. By the way, honey, let me know how your finances are. I enclose a check for 10 pounds for Santa Claus."

And he invited her thoughts about selling his beloved car, a Riley Kestrel that had been mothballed during the war, and putting the money into her account "against a rainy day."

He concluded, "Well my sweetheart this has been somewhat of a ramble. Needless to say, I miss you and David [whom he—aaargh—called Dumpling!] terribly."

1935 Riley Kestrel like the one my father stored during the war

He had been promoted to Wing Commander, roughly the equivalent of lieutenant colonel, at the beginning of the war; but rather than being "invalided out" of the Air Force, and being unfit for flying duties, he was posted to the Air Ministry in London to "fly a desk" as he put it, and we rented an apartment at 40 DeVere Gardens, a small street abutting the Royal Albert Hall. At the end of the road was High Street Kensington along which London buses 52 and 73 went on their way respectively to Mill Hill and to Stoke Newington. Curiously, those route numbers still exist today.

A Churchillian Spirit of Optimism

In those days one could see the smartly dressed drivers

and conductors of these buses with their impeccably creased jackets and pants and quasi-military caps, perhaps a holdover from the recently ended war which was celebrated by wild crowds outside Buckingham Palace. At that time, I was a gangly six-year-old in short pants and for whom my mother had hired what was then known as a nanny who was delegated to accompany me to the noisy crowd celebrating the end of the war. From our perch among thousands of spectators near the gates of Buckingham Palace, we could spy the balcony on which a smiling and waving King George VI, his wife Elizabeth,and his daughters Princess Elizabeth and Princess Margaret stood.

Soon after our sojourn at DeVere Gardens, my parents moved somewhat upscale to No. 1 Queen's Gate Place in South Kensington. In the same building, which, incidentally, boasted an elevator, were the only aristocrats I had seen up close: the Marquis and Marchioness of Sligo—Denis and José—who became lifelong friends of my parents. Their son Jeremy, Earl of Altamont, who later went on to serve as the squire of their family home in county Mayo, Ireland, was one of two playmates of mine during our stay in London.

Another was Camillus Travers, only son of P. L. (Pamela) Travers, the author of Mary Poppins. Pamela's fame, or notoriety, stemmed not only from her stern but friendly heroine, but she also wrote novels, and even some erotica. She never married but had two sons, one of whom she kept in London; the other was dispatched, even exiled, to Ireland, not to return and reunite with his brother until the age of 17. Pamela had lovers of both sexes and her little mews cottage was always alive with hard-to-find exotic food and drink, and even once a year on November 5 a boisterous party and bonfire to celebrate Guy Fawkes Day, a holiday celebrating the failure of Guy Fawkes' Gunpowder Plot to assassinate King James I in 1605.

My buddy Camillus and I roamed among the skeletal bombed-out buildings of London. Many years later, the *Mary Poppins* movie was released, which had brought Pamela into a contentious arrangement with Walt Disney because of what she perceived as his saccharine description of Mary Poppins. It starred Julie Andrews as well as Dick Van Dyke, who gave what many critics felt was the very worst attempt at a cockney accent ever seen—or heard. Another movie was the Bob Hope film *Road to Rio*, and so we were doubly delighted when we learned that Bob Hope, even though he had emigrated to the United States and made his career there, was British by birth.

During our stay in London, I attended the Lycée de Londres where all lessons were in French. I believe this is where my Francophilia took root. London at that time was a mess. There were great gaping holes where once there had been buildings, and one could see on interior walls open to the sky the outlines of staircases and fireplaces. The city had taken a terrible pounding from German aircraft, and later from the infamous V1 and V2 rockets that Londoners jauntily dubbed doodlebugs. Moreover, Winston Churchill had lost the 1945 election to the Labor Party of Clement Attlee, the country was broken and exhausted, and there was heavy taxation, rationing, general privation, and a pervasive down-at-heels feeling. The Labor Party won by two million votes, a slap in the face to

Britain's wartime hero Winston Churchill, whose inspiring rhetoric had spurred them on to victory.

From London, we moved in 1947 to the suburb of New Malden at the city's outer fringes, near Wimbledon in Surrey, where my parents had bought a small semi-detached house. My father also acquired a pre-war Morris 8 car which, like most British cars of the era, boasted neither heater nor radio. From that house I trudged daily to a pre-prep school called The Study, which was run by two elderly ladies and where the instruction was rudimentary at best.

At the end of my father's tour of duty at the Air Ministry, he was posted to an air force maintenance unit at Hullavington in Wiltshire, a town almost equidistant from the historical cities of Chippenham and Malmesbury; the latter was home to Alfred the Great in his fight against the Vikings.

The following year, at age eight, I was dispatched—like many upper- and middle-class children—to boarding school. My parents had put my name down for Winchester College, a prestigious and intellectually rigorous private—or in UK parlance, public—school, founded in 1382, among whose famous alumni are at least two prime ministers and many well-known authors. But my godfather was able to twist their arms and persuade them to send me to his alma mater instead, a Roman Catholic institution at Weybridge, in Surrey. My father, although nominally Catholic—and his sister Ethel, in Canada, was a nun—was hardly a devout one. Growing up, I seem to remember that he always claimed some kind of ailment or injury when it came time to go to Sunday Mass. My mother was Church of England. While they had married in a Catholic

Church, she had had to promise to bring up her children as God-fearing Papists.

3

BOARDING SCHOOL BLUES:
A DICKENSIAN RELIGIOUS EDUCATION

"Please Sir, I want some more ..."
–Charles Dickens

THE SCHOOL I ATTENDED was a notch below the top Catholic public schools in the UK—Ampleforth, Douai, Downside, and Stonyhurst. Nonetheless, each of them, as well as inculcating a solid and unwavering Catholicism, represented some of the dying embers of British imperialism: cut glass accents, and even an internal class system that separated boarders from day students. So, there I was, a little boy of eight in my brand-new school uniform with beanie cap and shorts, apprehensively sitting in the living room waiting for the Marquis to pick me up while apprehensively listening to the clock on the mantelpiece ticking away the time. That same clock graced my parents' living rooms for decades thereafter.

The priests at the school were of the Josephite order—sort of poor man's Jesuits. Their religiosity was narrow and unwavering. We rose at seven, said prayers kneeling on our beds, washed, dressed, and walked single file to morning mass. This was followed by a breakfast of indescribable paucity and stodginess—not quite at the thin gruel level that Oliver Twist endured, but not far from it. Confessions, communion, saints' feast days, and benedictions were all part of the doctrinal mix. I was hardly an *enfant terrible*, but on more than one occasion I called into question the priests' certitude, inquiring as to whether they had received any instruction in such religions as Judaism, Islam, or Buddhism.

I never received any satisfactory answer to this precocious exercise in journalism. They reminded me of the Church's naysaying when Galileo saw through his newly constructed telescope the moons of Jupiter—objects that circled another heavenly body—in direct disobedience of the Church's teaching. That teaching was even further refuted by Galileo's discovery that Venus circled the sun, not the Earth.

One reads in memoirs of others who have been similarly incarcerated about the shocking realities of public school life—corporal punishment, bullying, homoerotic behavior, and sadistic teachers. It's true that caning was administered at my school; something that I experienced only once and that quickly turned into a badge of honor. And some teachers did throw chalk at the stupid or inattentive, or cuffed their ears. As far as homoerotic behavior was concerned, I saw none of it save for once when I was in the infirmary with tonsillitis, being invited by a senior boy to inspect his erect penis, which I did with merely academic and distracted interest or what book reviewers used to call "mildly diverting." And we did hear some whispers of a master being dismissed for "playing around" with some of the pupils.

Discipline was very much *de rigueur* at the school; in fact, each week everyone received a four-inch by three-inch card with marks for tidiness, conduct and study. A total of 90–100 gained you a pink card—Very Good; between 70 and 90, a green one—Good; and under 70, a white one—Bad. One form of punishment, usually administered by a prefect, was the requirement to walk up and down for a prescribed period on a stretch of land abutting the playground. No euphemisms there about "Could Do Better." So much for notions of self esteem!

The school had an indifferent academic reputation, which I did nothing to enhance, shining if at all only in writin' and readin' but certainly not in 'rithmetic. Our English teacher was one Alan Hackney, the author of *I'm All Right, Jack* which was subsequently made into a movie starring Peter Sellers, and who drove an ancient London taxi, or Hackney Carriage. The school's athletic prowess was somewhat better, with rugby in the fall term, field hockey in the spring term, and cricket, of course, in the summer term. I shone at none of them, although I derived a small benefit on the cricket pitch where one of my equally bored teammates in the outfield explained the facts of life to me. I was incredulous that anyone could do that, least of all my father who was then about 40, and surely, I thought, well past having any procreative ability or inclination. But I was disabused of that uncharitable thought when my brother Richard was born.

Surviving Boarding School

In an article in *The Economist* titled, "Sad little boys: the backlash against Britain's boarding schools," the author noted that such schools are "odd places providing English upper-class boys with a blend of architectural beauty and physical discomfort with neoclassical corridors and cold showers and lashings of Latin and just plain lashings." Of the 57 British prime ministers, 20 went to one of the topflight schools— Eton. Perhaps the most profound threat to boarding schools, *The Economist* wrote, is more fundamental: sending a child as young as seven or eight away from home is not a privilege but a brutality.

Mercifully, I was able to escape some of that later, at Magee University in Ireland where the Irish allowed escape from notions of empire and exclusivity; and at King Alfred School in Germany where the place was totally free of class distinctions or religious indoctrination, and one would certainly not dare to inflict on a defeated nation any idea of *snobbisme* or victorious superiority.

The great thing about the school, though, was that it gave me a lifelong love of reading. For once one had finished the allotted "prep" or homework, there was no home to go to and no escaping from the room. The only recourse was to read —and the room was lined with the works of Scott, Dickens, Conrad, and other classical authors. Besides these, I've had a lifelong "always a book on the go" approach to reading with particular favorites being George Orwell, Harold Nicholson, and Christopher Hitchens.

At school, I was part of a small rebel faction that kicked around a soccer ball during the rugby term. Which brings me to Wolverhampton. The town where my father was stationed is in the English midlands and boasted a soccer team, Wolverhampton Wanderers, "the Wolves," that was stellar. They topped the first division table, won the FA Cup, and were the first professional team to install floodlights and to challenge European clubs from Hungary and the Soviet Union; their captain Billy Wright captained the England team, and their goalkeeper Bert Williams was England's goalie, and later ennobled for charitable work. Best of all, their left winger Jimmy Mullen coached the local RAF team which meant that when I was home from school for Christmas and Easter vacations, I got to sit in the directors' box and to meet my footballing heroes at the end of a match.

During the half century since then, the Wolves sank to the English fourth division, went bankrupt, were rescued by millionaire industrialist Sir Jack Hayward, and are now back in the premier division. I have supported them throughout that time and have even donned on occasion their gold and black shirt. Other members of my and my wife Shelly's family have joined this phalanx of Wolves supporters, Sam and Jennifer in particular.

Also, at this time, I gained some precarious brownie points when my father flew me in a single engine plane, a Percival Prentice. This was a plane described by the *Classic Aircraft Trust* as being the object of an unkind saying that it "doesn't so much climb as truncle along the runway until the curvature of the earth makes the ground fade away. She has a distinct disapproval of rush, but she's immensely strong and reliable, and the cockpit is bigger than that of a London taxi. She might not get there fast," the Trust continued, "but she'll never let you down. The aircraft first flew in 1946 and served the RAF as a basic trainer until 1953."

Percival Prentice trainer of the type my father took me up in when I was 8

In 1952, my father was posted to Germany for the post-WWII Allied occupation and, following the summer term at my English school, I flew to Cologne in a DC-3 of British European Airways to join my parents.

4

POSTWAR GERMANY:
OUT OF THE ASHES AND RUBBLE

"In the midst of chaos, there is also opportunity."
—Sun Tzu, The Art of War

BEFORE EMBARKING on my five year sojourn in Germany, I should reference the magisterial work *Aftermath* by Harold Jahner and whose subtitle is *Life in the Fallout of the Third Reich 1945 to 1955.*

The book is described as "a revelatory history of the transformational decade that followed World War II, when Germany raised itself out of the ashes of defeat, turned away from fascism, and reckoned with the corruption of its soul and the horrors of the Holocaust." The book received wide acclaim and spent 48 weeks on the bestseller list in Germany when it was published there. From the dust jacket:

"The years 1945 to 1955 were a raw and wild decade that found many Germans politically, economically and morally bankrupt. Victorious allied forces occupied the four zones that made up postwar Germany. More than half the population was displaced; 10 million newly released forced laborers and several million prisoners of war returned to an uncertain existence. Cities lay in ruins—no mail, no trains, no traffic—with bodies yet to be found beneath the towering rubble. *Aftermath* is the first history of Germany's national mentality in the immediate postwar years. This decade is portrayed as a period that proved decisive for Germany's future and one starkly different from how most of us imagine it today. *Aftermath* helps to answer the question: how does a nation recover from fascism and turn toward a free society once more."

I spent most of my teenage years in that same Germany and was privileged to observe much of what Janner had to say about the country beginning to rise from the ashes of a truly dreadful war.

My initial impressions of Germany were distinctly negative. Why would they not be? As a child in wartime Wales, I had heard the terrifying rants of Hitler on the radio, and had heard Winston Churchill's combative Germanophobe oratory. This was fighting talk. Yes, Germany was a land of civility and culture, a country that had produced Goethe and

Beethoven; but now its barbarian forces were busy trying to bomb Britain into submission. "We are resolved to destroy Hitler and every vestige of the Nazi regime," said Churchill. "We will never negotiate with Hitler or any of his gang." He went on to describe the German dictator as a "bloodthirsty guttersnipe." No wonder we were anti-German: our soldiers and airmen were getting killed or wounded on the ground and in the air. And we learned a little of the horrors perpetrated upon millions of Jews.

I was supposed to continue at high school to age 18, but at the end of the summer term of 1952, at age 13, I left without much regret for the last time and joined my parents in Germany where my father had been posted to a maintenance unit at the RAF station.

The flight from London to Germany in a DC-3 of what was then British European Airways landed at Royal Air Force Station, Wahn, which also served as the civil airport for Cologne-Bonn. It was a beautiful summer day. My parents' house was on Mulheimer Strasse in the village of Troisdorf, population of 76,000, whose first large settlements go back to the 9th and 10th century. The city is twinned with Corfu, Greece. Among its notable denizens were John Sibirich (1476 –1554), a pioneering printer and friend of Erasmus.

Our new home was 16 miles from Cologne, and had been commandeered from a high-ranking German executive named Hans Klefisch at a nearby dynamite factory. What a name for someone swimming in the fetid waters of Nazism. And what a contrast it was to the little semi-detached house in the London suburbs that we'd moved to from central London in 1948! This was a mansion, situated well back from the road, with large airy rooms, distinctly un-British plumbing including a bidet, and expansive gardens in which there were luxuriant trees and bushes, abundant fruits—even grapes.

There was a maid, Heidi, who was engaged to be married and who carried with her wherever her chores in the house took her, a very explicit preparation for the nuptials ahead titled *Vas Jeden Frau Wissen Muss—What Every Woman Should Know*. There was also a cook and a gardener, and my father had a driver pick him up each morning in a shiny Opel car to go to the air force base where he headed something called a Maintenance Unit, a far cry from his days piloting warplanes. And best of all, after the rationing and privations of postwar Britain, there were wonderful and varied foods to be found in the local German shops where my mother practiced her primitive German to generally very receptive tradespeople.

Soon after my arrival, my mother accompanied me to the plaza surrounding the beautiful and largely unharmed cathedral at Cologne, a building visible from miles around and dating from the 13th century, and where less than two years later my sister Elizabeth would be christened. We sat in the sun drinking *apfelsinen*—fizzy apple juice—and were surrounded by the contrasting scene of seemingly animated and relaxed denizens of that city, the bombed and useless Ludendorf Bridge that had partly fallen into the river Rhine, and the skeletons of buildings, many of whose facades were pockmarked with bullet holes.

Shortly afterwards, my father dropped his own bombshell of sorts. I was to be sent to King Alfred School, a

Cologne Cathedral intact among devastation surrounding it—note upper left railway bridge collapsed in the Rhine

boarding school in Schleswig-Holstein, the northernmost state in Germany, for the sons—and heavens—daughters(!) of UK forces personnel.

The school's headmaster was the war hero Sir Frederick Spencer-Chapman, author of *The Jungle is Neutral*, a book about his wartime exploits in what is now Malaysia.

During the war, Spencer-Chapman had organized parties of trained guerrilla forces that would have delayed the Japanese invasion of Singapore. He speculated that the effect of the trained forces he led would have delayed the Japanese invasion long enough for British reinforcements to arrive in Singapore, and Singapore might not have fallen. Much more to the point, though, for this history, is that this would have meant that my father's life would have turned out dramatically differently in that he would have evaded capture by the Japanese and therefore escaped his three-and-a-half year incarceration.

Sir Frederick Spencer-Chapman

Spencer-Chapman had attended the spartan Scottish school Gordonstoun, the rigorous school in North Scotland that Prince Charles attended as a young boy and described in highly negative terms. While at Gordonstoun, Spencer-Chapman was influenced by the school's founder and head, Kurt Hahn, and his ideals of service, character, and discipline. Spencer-Chapman infused these ideals he had learned into the King Alfred School ethos and was ideally suited as an adventurer and commando to take his place at the head of this unique scholastic experiment. Despite my initial horror at attending such a school, it became one of the most significant influences in my life's journey.

Spencer-Chapman continued his career with the headmastership of a school in South Africa. He suffered from frequent and severe back pain, as well as recurring stomach pain and headaches. He committed suicide in his study on 8 August 1971, leaving a note for his wife reading, "I don't want you to have to nurse an invalid for the rest of my life."

5

KING ALFRED SCHOOL PLÖN:
A VIBRANT SCHOOL IN A DEFEATED GERMANY

*"Do not forget, that it is not brilliance and cleverness that
get you to the top in the world, but reliability, steadiness,
goodness, kindness—all that we call character."*
*–Sir Frederick Spencer-Chapman, headmaster at King Alfred
School (excerpt from the Red Dragon school magazine)*

THE SCHOOL WAS NOTHING LIKE I HAD EVER
experienced at my Catholic boarding school in England. The
school facilities, which had served as Hitler's deputy Admiral
Doenitz's submarine officer training establishment, were
located some 450 miles north of Cologne at Plön, in Schleswig-
Holstein between Lubeck and Kiel, about 50 miles south of the
Danish border.

I was horrified. But I had no choice, and in September
1952, I boarded a train at Cologne along with other "service

brats" headed to King Alfred School. The privately chartered train wound its way through Dusseldorf, Essen, Dortmund, Hannover, Bremen, Hamburg, and on up to Plön. At each stop, more students, ages 13 to 18, came aboard. It is difficult to describe the scenes of utter devastation that we passed through. Industrial cities such as Essen, home of the Krupp steelworks, had been virtually flattened by British and American bombing.

Air Chief Marshall Sir Arthur Travers ("Bomber") Harris had singled out the four cities designated as "industrial targets"—Cologne, Essen, Dortmund and Duisburg—for particularly severe attacks. In 1942 alone, Harris had launched 1,500 bombing sorties against Essen. On a single night in the following year, some 700 RAF planes attacked the city. The so-called "thousand bomber raids" by the US Air Force in daylight, and the RAF at night, inflicted huge loss of life and massive damage on the area in general, and on Essen in particular. The city was virtually obliterated.

As we schoolchildren observed the devastation, our attitude was pretty much, "Well, they got what they deserved." We had, after all, been fully inculcated with anti-German sentiments. We even—and this was unforgivable at the time, and would be even more so now—leaned from the train window as we steamed through Hamburg station at morning rush hour, and sang an inverted version of the German national anthem: *"Deutschland, Deutschland unter alles; Deutschland, Deutschland ist kaput ..."* ("Germany, Germany, under all, Germany, Germany is broken ...")

It was curious to see, considering Germany's incredible advances in the last few decades, the remarkable recent speech in the Bundestag by Britain's new king Charles III—and appropriately in impeccable German, a tribute not only to his hosts but also a tip of the hat to his German ancestors.

We were met at Plön railway station by a fleet of buses driven by dark-green-suited German members of the Control Commission for Germany (CCG), a force of workers under the control of the British military and composed of drivers, kitchen staff, cleaners, etc. As we rolled through the school gates, we sang songs about our imminent incarceration but surely less inflammatory than those we'd sung on the train in Hamburg.

We were all pretty much aware of King Alfred School's brief and unique history. The school had opened in May 1948 as a co-educational boarding school for the children of the British Armed Forces and Control Commission personnel stationed in the British zone of postwar Germany. It was situated on the shores of the Grosser Plöner See, in a beautiful area of hills and woods often called Holstein, Switzerland. The town of Plön was founded in 1236 when the Free City of Lubeck—some 25 kilometers away—granted it a charter. Thirty kilometers north of Plön lies Kiel, formerly one of Germany's greatest naval bases, and it was natural therefore that the German naval authorities, seeking to accommodate the steadily expanding German Navy, should turn to the strip of land on the Plöner See to build a naval barracks. By April 1938, all the buildings on the estate were completed and the training of German naval personnel began.

In February 1940, the German Navy's ever-expanding submarine arm decided to establish at Plön its No 1 U-boat Training School. While the U-boat crews trained at Plön, strange experiments were taking place at the southern end of the Grosser Plöner See—experiments involving long concrete ramps, highly inflammable fuel, and mysterious small aircraft. The V-I rocket, a pilotless bomb, was being tried out and the barracks must have been awash with rumors of the promised secret weapon that was intended to do so much to tip the scales of the war in Germany's favor.

After the failure of the Ardennes offensive in December 1944, on the Western Front, and with the Eastern Front liable to crack at any moment, the German Navy's headquarters moved to Plön in March 1945. No doubt the connection to Plön of Admiral Karl Dönitz, Hitler's designated successor, gave the barracks new prominence during the last weeks of the war. Within a few days of the end of the war, however, the British 6th Guards Tank Brigade set up its headquarters in the barracks and a few weeks later, the Royal Navy took over those barracks from the Guards and was then named HMS Royal Alfred, thus pointing the way to the school's title.

To say that the British Forces Education Service (BFES) then commandeered it is to ignore the most strenuous efforts and perseverance on the part of the director in wresting this magnificent property from the armed forces so that a boarding school might be established there. April of 1948, the month before the school was due to open, was a time of feverish activity. Outside, the Garrison Engineer supervised the various structural alterations, surprisingly few in fact, needed to convert fine barracks buildings into unrivaled school buildings.

All That We Call Character

The 600 or so boys and girls aged 11 to 18 were accommodated in five double houses, 50 to 60 in each house. Each house had a housemaster with three or four male assistant teachers, and a house mistress with three or four assistants. Selected seniors were called Helpers, not Prefects, their role being one of leadership and mentoring rather than simply of authority.

The houses were named Churchill, Roosevelt, Temple (after the archbishop), Fleming (after the discoverer of penicillin), and Nansen (after the Norwegian arctic explorer), which is where I was for the duration. Rivalry between houses was intense in all sports and activities. There were teaching and craft blocks, assembly and dining halls, a double gym, track and playing fields, a "hospital" block, stables with indoor riding ring, boathouses, garages, a rifle range, sick bay, and lodgings for unmarried teachers.

The school had a Church of England chapel and a Catholic one. Apart from the teaching staff there was also an Anglican Chaplain, matrons in all the houses and "hospital," sometimes a school doctor, dentist and Combined Cadet Force (CCF)) officer, and seven British administrative staff. German staff were also numerous: teachers (of German, horseback riding, physical education, music, sailing), porters, matrons, clerks, drivers, mechanics, gardeners, cooks, waiters, and a barber.

Despite the war having ended a mere three years earlier, the German staff were at once given equal respect and worked hard and loyally. British staff had to serve a probationary year; if they could not stand the hectic pace (or the tax and duty-free gin and whisky), their contract was ended.

In 1952, his last year as headmaster of the school, Sir Frederick Spencer-Chapman, in the *Red Dragon*, King Alfred School's official publication, reported:

> "The scope of the wonderful experiment that has gone on here... providing an opportunity not only for one privileged class but for a complete cross-section of the community. The public schools at home have a long and splendid tradition, he said, but they have one nationality, one sex, one religion and in general one income group. Here we have 20 nationalities, half a dozen religions and boys and girls of every sort of income and background and every kind of aptitude and ability. We have produced here a living community where children of all kinds can move with disciplined self-confidence, are treated as individuals and are given every opportunity to make the most of whatever talents they have.
>
> "Do not forget, that it is not brilliance and cleverness that get you to the top in the world, but reliability, steadiness, goodness, kindness—all that we call character."

To allow plenty of light for sports, lessons were from 9 am till lunchtime, and then from 5 pm to 7 pm in winter and from 2 pm to 4 pm in summer. There was a compulsory rest period after lunch. A major feature was the enormous enthusiasm given to sports and activities. Unlike St George's, where basically it was rugby in the autumn term, field hockey in the spring term, and cricket in the summer term, KAS also offered riding, sailing, boxing, rifle shooting, country dancing, skating and skiing in season, printing, Scouts and Guides, Army cadet force with summer camp, inter-house music and verse-speaking competitions.

The school intercom was used for evening news bulletins, talks, and the occasional play. Memorable school theatrical productions in the large assembly hall, which was also a fully equipped theatre, included "Macbeth," "Toad of Toad Hall," "Peer Gynt," and "Pygmalion."

The school won the Milocarian Trophy (for athletics in British schools) from 1952 to 1956 and again in 1957—six times in its short life of a dozen years. For economic reasons totally unrelated to the prowess of KAS, the school closed in 1959. Alas, now the only records of this inspirational school are in the old copies of the *Red Dragon*, the school magazine published each term, and in the vaults of the War Office or Foreign Office, but the school lives on in the minds and memories of the Wyvern Club: the one hundred or so former pupils and staff who meet in London each year on the first Saturday in January.

Most Likely To Succeed?

Despite my initial misgivings about KAS, it was an extraordinary experience: the school was classless in that we were the children of generals and corporals and everything in between, and nonsexist in that girls were totally the equal of boys even in that pre-emancipation era. Notable alumni included actresses Helen Ryan and Susannah York. I wish I could report that I was the "most likely to succeed." I scraped onto a place in the House soccer team, made sergeant in the cadet force, and became a Helper and eventually Head Boy of my House.

Academically, I was a dud at math and science, but did well at English and history. Even though I've had a lifelong love of thoroughbred horse racing, I was a sad sack in the school's horseback riding programs. In fact, the riding instructor, a fearsome former Prussian cavalry officer who wore a monocle and jackboots, would frequently shout, "Voods: you look like booter on hot potato on dat horse."

My theatrical career was equally undistinguished: I played the third murderer in Macbeth and a Troll in Peer Gynt. However, there was reflected light in the former, where Lady Macbeth was played by Helen Ryan who went on to a stellar movie and television career with roles that included Elizabeth I and Edward VII's wife, Alexandra.

The change from an all-boys' school with execrable food, rigid rules and force-fed Catholicism to a still rigorous but easy-going co-ed institution with kids from all classes and backgrounds was extraordinary. The chefs were former employees of the Hamburg America shipping line, as were the white-coated waiters, and the food, with the offerings posted on menu boards outside the dining hall, was of the highest quality, and included such German delicacies as labskaus, sauerkraut, and various types of schnitzels. We played soccer against local German teams, and while there was none of that "it's not whether you win or lose but how you played the game" mentality, we were friendly with the local lads even after pulling out all the stops to win against them.

Among our adversaries were students of the local Schloss, a noted private school in the town of Plön, founded in 1704 as a Latin school and renamed in 1867 as the Königlich Preusisches Gymnasium. It looks back to a rich and colorful checkered history of more than 300 years. Sports included soccer, which they played against King Alfred school. We would also hold debates and dances with them. My memory is of them—confident, blond, heel-clicking, well-groomed, impeccably mannered—and of us: unsophisticated, unsure, callow.

But we did date the KAS girls, and in a way that would be considered hopelessly naive today. We walked, sometimes daringly hand in hand, to classes, to meals, or to sports events; but there was no serious kissing, no groping, and certainly no sex.

In my last but one term, I shared a room with a chap named Peter Willis, a Yorkshireman. Somehow or other we were able to acquire cigarettes, and we would toss the butts out of the dormer window onto the sloping roof. In winter, these fell into the snow; but when Spring came, we were aghast to see the collection of butts open to full view and scrambled to clear them. As with many of my contemporaries, Peter went to the Royal Military Academy at Sandhurst; but as a 33-year-old captain in the famous Green Howards, a Yorkshire regiment, he was shot and killed by a sniper in Northern Ireland during the time that was known as "The Troubles," also called a "Northern Ireland conflict," a violent sectarian battle from about 1968 to 1998 between the overwhelmingly Protestant unionists (loyalists), who wanted the province to remain part of the United Kingdom, and the overwhelmingly Roman Catholic nationalists (republicans), who wanted Northern Ireland to become part of the Republic of Ireland.

My closest friend at Plön was Michael Minhall, an accomplished sportsman and a brilliant and creative comedian and mimic. Some years after leaving the school, we shared an apartment in London for a year before tiring of each other's cooking and our largely pathetic efforts to get dates, even in then "swinging" London—the London of Carnaby Street, miniskirts, the Mini, and the Beatles.

I had passed the exams for Sandhurst, the military equivalent of West Point. The curious interview procedure was pretty much straight out of the Boer War: ramrod straight officer-types putting candidates through initiatives in fording rivers, jumping stone walls and later checking to discern if you were a gentleman, attacking meals with the correct fork, etc. English, math, and current affairs were mandatory, and I had picked French and history as electives. Results were respectable. Even after cramming day and night for the math test, I scraped by the pass mark with a razor thin margin. Nevertheless, I subsequently learned that I came out 58th out of 2,000 candidates.

A contemporary of mine and somewhat of a hero was Bill Cornock, who was at King Alfred School and head of

Nansen House, and was one of those "most likely to succeed" students. He excelled at pretty much everything, and after Sandhurst and his stellar career, rose through the officer ranks to become a Brigadier General. He went on to that great military reward, being decorated with such honors as the CBE and OBE and dying last year in his 80s. I often wonder if that might have been me, had I taken that road.

6

OUTWARD BOUND:
LEADERSHIP IN THE ROUGH

"There is more in us than we know."
–Kurt Hahn

EVEN THOUGH I'D DEMONSTRATED that I was apparently "officer material," I decided that the army would be better off without me—and vice versa. I think I was too much of a free thinker to have been constrained by military life. The road not taken, yes? This did not please my military father, who chose not to fund the university degree course I'd decided to embark upon. His parsimony could easily have led to feelings of deprivation on my part. In fact, if anything, it was a wakeup call to make the most of what I did have. Just think, if I had gone on to Sandhurst I might have wound up in the same regiment as my former roommate, Peter Willis, and suffered his same fate.

In the time between the Sandhurst exams and starting university, at least my father coughed up enough money to send me on a month's course at the Outward Bound School in the Lake District of Northwest England to toughen me up. It was February of 1957 and, as is even more usual in that part of Britain than in the rest of it, the weather was cold, damp, and rainy.

There were about 30 of us on the course. We were awakened at 6 am, donned only shorts, and ran the quarter mile or so around the tarn, or mountain lake. At the end point we stripped off the shorts and dove into the freezing water, watched closely by the Italian maids in the nearby mansion that served the less rigorous aspects of the experience. These included map-reading, orienteering, and lessons on survival in the local inhospitable landscape. We climbed rocks, did rope work, ran races, sailed kayaks—the whole thing culminating in a three-man, three-day expedition with bivouacs and army-style rations, one of which I led. This was a competition to see how many cairns (little piles of rock in the mountains containing cans with messages in them) we could reach in the shortest time. The Outward Bound motto incidentally had echoes of Plön: "To serve, to strive and not to yield." Upon returning to London buff and fit, I immediately came down with a serious cold and took to bed for a week or two.

Before setting off for university, I had dated an "older woman" who was 22 to my 18. She was Danish, and was studying in England in the household of a Danish family. A member of that family had phoned my mother noting that since

I was a "young English gentleman," I might like to escort Inge, a tall blonde and beautiful Dane, to the movies, restaurants, and the like. She also had the use of the family car. I was happy to oblige.

Sometime later I was invited to visit her in Copenhagen. I had saved up the requisite 10 pounds for the trip by boat from Harwich in the East Coast of England to the Hook of Holland. From there I boarded the Holland Scandinavia Express which steamed through Holland, Belgium, and parts of Germany, even nudging close to King Alfred School, now no longer an academic institution but a revived German naval school.

The journey was an adventure: taking in a couple of islands with each stop, punctuated by groaning tables of extraordinary Danish food, including the famous *smorrebröd.* Inge met me at Copenhagen's central station, and whisked me to her parents' apartment on the Roskildevej.

And what a welcome and a greeting that was: lots of good food, beer, and numerous toasts in English and in Danish, including the famous toast; *dien scholl; mien scholl; ala vackra flicker scholl*—roughly, "Cheers to me and cheers to you and cheers to all the pretty girls."

My room in the apartment was spacious and elegant, containing all the appropriate male scents, and where Inge's father had thoughtfully placed a package of condoms. Ah Scandinavia! So much different from button-down England.

He also pressed wodges of *krone*, Danish money, into my hands and off we went to various sites in Copenhagen, often in trams driven, surprisingly to my untrained eye, by women (I had never seen a woman drive a tram, or indeed a bus!) and to the Atlantic Palace and other nightclubs in the city, as well as the famous Tivoli gardens. We visited various museums, the Carlsberg and Tuborg breweries, and Hamlet's famous castle at Elsinore.

He even floated the idea of my joining his company. Aha, another road not taken. But alas, absence apparently does not make the heart grow fonder, and after the wonderful adventure in Denmark, I did not encounter Inge again. Indeed, a sad parting, mutually agreed.

7

MAGEE UNIVERSITY COLLEGE:
18 YEARS OLD AND ON MY OWN

"Success is to be measured not so much by the position that one has reached in life as by the obstacles which one has overcome."
–Booker T. Washington

AT THAT TIME in the UK, university tuition was free; but one still had to find money for board and lodging, books, etc. So, I discovered Magee University College in Londonderry, Northern Ireland, a two-year feeder college for Trinity College, Dublin, and Queen's University, Belfast with reasonable fees for room and food. This was a road taken with enthusiasm. I chose to go the Trinity route—a renowned university founded by Queen Elizabeth I in 1592 as a bastion of Protestantism in a sea of papists. Among its alumni were Jonathan Swift, Edmund Burke, Oscar Wilde, Samuel Beckett, and Oliver Goldsmith.

Good enough, I thought, for an aspiring teacher of English.

Magee University College, Londonderry, Northern Ireland

And so, in the fall of 1958, I set off from Liverpool, on the deck, not a cabin, of a boat that had seen its best days, for the overnight voyage to Derry (some 200 miles) where we steamed into harbor on a cold and foggy early September morning.

I was 18, and pretty much on my own in the sense that I'd have to work during vacations. Since there was little opportunity for that in Northern Ireland, I would certainly have to hitchhike to and from London or other big English cities. And this I did, going from Londonderry through Belfast and Dublin, taking the ferry across to Wales, and continuing down to London. There, I held jobs as a barman, market gardener, factory worker, and bookstore clerk (as a gopher for the owner of Foyles famous London bookstore) before reversing the journey and going back to college. I have vivid memories of running through the deserted streets of Belfast in the early morning during a time of what became known as "The Troubles." Hitchhiking was certainly not the dangerous enterprise it is today; in fact, many of the drivers I encountered on my journeys by thumb over a 500-mile hike were engaging and amiable souls.

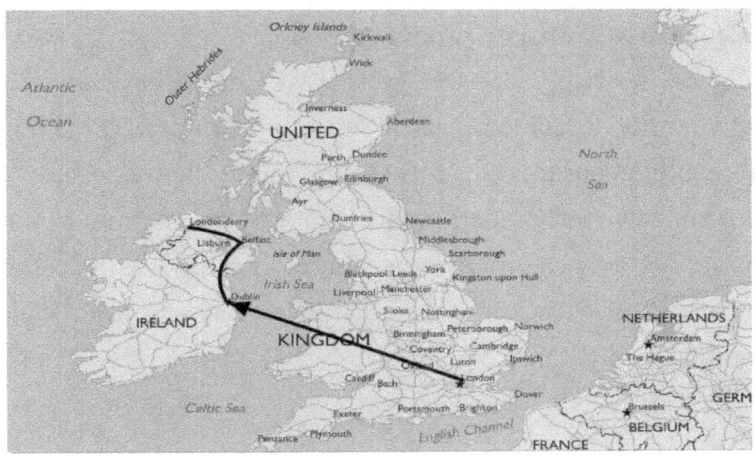

My 500-mile hitchhiking journey from Magee University College to London and back again for summer work.

At Magee, I was "reading"—the UK college term for studying—English, particularly the restoration playwrights Goldsmith, Wycherly, Congreve, Farquar, and Sheridan. I loved this stuff, but also spent a lot of my time in extracurricular activities. These included the presidency of the Overseas Students Society, the Debating Society, and the History Society. I also played soccer for the college (compensating for the lack of that sport at my first boarding school).

The debating gig was a high point in my Magee University career. It involved donning a tuxedo and traveling to debates at Trinity College Dublin, University College Dublin, and Queen's University Belfast. Besides being an intellectual exercise and challenge, it was a wonderful way to get to know the people of both Northern Ireland and the Republic of Ireland—two remarkably different entities. Some considerable time later, I would study for and gain a PhD at Northern Ireland's Ulster University, one of whose constituent colleges is Magee. Full circle, yes?

After two years, the point at which I should have gone on to Trinity, I decided that the financial situation had become untenable; accordingly, I left the university. It was a blow, to be sure, but "out of darkness cometh light," and as a result of my decent performance at Magee, I was swiftly offered a position as a teacher of English in a prep school in Wales. Another road taken.

8

PREP SCHOOL TEACHER:
SHADES OF EVELYN WAUGH'S *DECLINE AND FALL*

"Have you at any time been detained in a mental home or
similar institution? If so, give particulars."
–Evelyn Waugh, Decline and Fall

AFTER LEAVING MAGEE, I was uncertain about how
I wanted to spend my life. My original intention in going
to university was to become a teacher. Now, degreeless, I
seriously wondered if that was a viable option. But what else
to do? Private preparatory schools were short of teachers; my
academic performance at Magee had been pretty good, so I
went to the scholastic agents with the Dickensian name of
Gabbitas and Thring. There I learned that there was a vacancy
at a boys' preparatory school in North Wales. I applied, and
the headmaster phoned me to ask if I could bowl into the right

cricket net. This seemed like an odd set of priorities; nonetheless, I apparently answered the question to his satisfaction, and he promptly offered me 90 pounds, although I was uncertain whether this amount was per term or per year. The amount, however, was supplemented by free accommodation, meals, and laundry.

Thus, armed with the prospect of gainful employment, I boarded a train in London for the 250-mile journey to North Wales that chugged through Holyhead. Arriving at the station of Llandudno, I was met by the deputy headmaster who lost no time in informing me that I was in fact a very poor second choice. (What, again?) The man first offered the job had apparently backed out at the last minute. The deputy was a man of saturnine appearance with slicked back hair and a reptilian look. He had used part of a small inheritance to buy a small share in the school. There, he taught French with a decidedly Manchester intonation.

My colleagues were right out of Evelyn Waugh's *Decline and Fall*, a comic novel about being a master at a prep school in Wales. The math master drove a 1926 Rolls Royce and smoked so much that, instead of flicking the ash off his cigarette with his fingers, he would simply toss his head with the cigarette still in his mouth so that the ash dropped to the floor. Another was a retired naval commander who would issue ship's whistle noises from his bedroom which adjoined the masters' common room. "Just going astern, old boy," he would inform the curious. The battered van, in which he journeyed to the nearby village to purchase provisions, he dubbed the jolly boat.

The other lesson I took from my prep school colleagues was an introduction to horse racing. This has been a lifelong enthusiasm (road taken and continued), taking me and later my American wife Shelly to some 14 race tracks in England, Wales, the US, Canada, France, and even Barbados. As a journalist, this enabled a temporary abandonment of medical journalism and the chance to interview not only such jockeys as Hall of Fame inductee Sandy Hawley but also the four women jockeys carving a newfound career in horse racing.

When people heard of my interest in this wonderful sport and inquired as to whether I made huge amounts of money at it, my typical response was that the outcome of races is pretty much up in the air mainly because those wonderful animals have not yet learned how to translate the form guide in the daily racing program. But I did have some skin in the game with a part interest years later in two horses, Reine des Lions and Mine for Love, both of which won races before being claimed.

Back at the prep school, before the official start of term time, I took the opportunity to explore the school grounds, the gym, and the pool, and overheard some of the gardening staff wondering whether I was a teacher or a new pupil. This did nothing to improve my already slender confidence or to help my incipient apprehensiveness.

Other characters at the school included a possibly shell-shocked World War II veteran who appeared to have only one set of clothes. He professed to wash up as far as possible on Monday; down as far as possible on Tuesday; and if possible on Wednesday. He ordered a pound of foul-smelling tobacco from Scotland each month. On Sports Day, always attended by a good number of the parents, Mr. Hobson, or Hobbo as he was known, appeared at the door of the staff room wearing a faded school blazer, an equally faded beanie school cap, a scarf around his neck, and a pair of rumpled gray pants bearing traces of urine. "I am dressed," he said, "pour le sport." The deputy headmaster was horrified. "Get him out of here before the parents see him," he hissed.

The headmaster himself was an enormously rotund clerical gentleman—the Rev. Starkey. He wandered about the school wearing a benign expression. He had an enormous bulge in his crotch which caused some of the younger staff members to invent some kind of vehicle that he could push in front of him in order to propel this weight forward. They variously suggested naming such a vehicle a bollock cart or a testicle tricycle. Another character in the school was Harry. Harry was the handyman and all-purpose factotum who cared little for rank or protocol. He would come to the staff room to light a fire and cheerily announce: "My bed was like a tent this morning, and I 'ad my old woman three times before breakfast." He was also heard to say that the reverend "'adn't seen it" since he was fourteen.

One influence at that time was a man twice my age—Keith Jones. Keith was the product of an excellent local private school, was extraordinarily well-read and well-spoken ... and highly opinionated. But he cared little for material success and earned his living selling cars at a dealership a mile or so away from the tiny semi-detached house where he lived with his wife Sheila.

The couple lived for ideas, the principal one of which was socialism. They railed at what they saw as the effete Conservative government of the day and were still smarting from the ill-advised British attack on Egypt when that country seized the Suez Canal. They weaned me from my own Tory notions, and from the Conservative *Times* newspaper to the more leftist *Guardian* and *Observer,* both of which editorialized against the Suez attack that led eventually to the resignation of Prime Minister Anthony Eden.

Keith and Sheila would pick me up at the school, and off we'd go to one of the local pubs, especially one named Maggie Murphy's that faced the Conwy estuary and the famous 13th century castle on its other side, and where, some 30 years later, I would propose to my American wife, Shelly.

There, over three or four pints of beer, we would talk politics way into the night. The pub's barman and manager was an affable soul and part time pedant. If you bellied up to the bar and ordered "same again" he would tut tut that you couldn't possibly have the same again since you've already had it and would be better off saying "similar."

The future for a teacher without traditional qualifications seemed rather constricted. I could of course have enrolled in some kind of part-time degree program, but there weren't many to be had, and anyway I was beginning to think that teaching itself was probably not what I wanted to do for the rest of my life, even though much later in life I did teach a course in medical writing. Maybe the business world would be the road to take, I thought, and headed to London.

9

LONDON IN THE SWINGING SIXTIES: FOOD, POLITICS, AND CAMARADERIE

"Oh, I love London society! It is entirely composed now of beautiful idiots and brilliant lunatics."
–Oscar Wilde

IN LONDON IN THE SIXTIES, a city of the mini skirt and the Beatles, having scanned the "situations vacant" column in the evening papers, I joined the Underwood Corporation as a writer of promotional and advertising copy and as a sales guy going out to schools to demonstrate the wonders of the relatively newly-invented electric typewriter.

I shared a tiny apartment—a room, really—with my old Plön buddy, Michael Minhall. For a year or so, while I worked in the daytime and he at night in the publishing business, we had an arrangement in which he cooked dinner when I came home, and

I cooked breakfast when he did. Otherwise, we probably visited every theater in London, including the Royal Court Theatre, just around the corner in Sloane Square, and several racetracks, as well as endlessly looking for girls. One of those, Georgina Allen, was a fix-up date. More about her later (a road about to be taken).

Ultimately, Michael and I tired of the not so haute cuisine. I had learned from another friend whose cousin, recently divorced, took in lodgers at her large Victorian house in Weybridge, 30 miles south of the capital and the site of my former school, St. George's. Moving there was the beginning of an unforgettable three years—my last in England.

Wendy, the woman who ran the house at Thames Street in Weybridge, wrote a regular column on cookery for a popular magazine called *My Home*. Opposite the house stood the Old Crown Inn, and beyond that the River Thames itself.

Wendy was also a part-time actress who took in lodgers to supplement her income: one was a former actor who had become a television executive; another was an engineer; a third was a Nigerian student; the fourth was a young woman who was an aspiring actress and who helped with the household chores; and I was the fifth. There were occasional *au pairs* from various Scandinavian countries, and the list was completed by Wendy's two young daughters.

The house was alive with liaisons, fabulous food, and equally wonderful conversation, mainly about politics for we were all middle-class fashionable socialists. As for the liaisons, Wendy was having an affair with the television executive, I had hooked up with Ms. Allen who came to the house regularly, and as for the food, photographers from the magazine would come to photograph dinner. Usually, one or more of us would have to be extricated from the Old Crown Inn beforehand so as to be on hand for Wendy's gastronomic inventions.

This ignited a lifetime enthusiasm for *haute cuisine*. Nothing fancy, mind you. I draw the line at sheep's eyeballs, for example. But French cuisine surely attracts my gastronomic attention with occasional infusions of British staples such as shepherd's pie.

No matter what time I arrived from London, there was always food and drink and talk and laughter. The television executive was a talented piano player and wit. By that time, I was working for Viners of Sheffield, a company that made sterling silver and silver-plated hollowware. They paid me well, gave me a car, and my job was to visit all the jewelers in London with my wares. Curiously, given that ultra-capitalistic activity, I and other members of the household became active members of the Labor Party, paying our dues every week. The house was always full of visitors and guests, including such luminaries as Fanny and Johnny Craddock, the famous husband and wife television chefs.

A Road to Politics?

In 1964, when Labor was about to come to power under Harold Wilson, after more than a decade of Conservative rule, the household set me up to run as a Labour candidate in municipal elections for the District of Walton on Thames, an area peopled almost entirely by stockbrokers, bankers, and well-to-do business folk. Since the district was almost entirely inhabited by people of Conservative persuasion it was quite predictable that I would lose. But I went at it with a will, knocking on doors and putting up signs that read "Vote Woods." In fact, although the Conservative won and the Liberal was relegated to last place, I managed to squeak through in second. Thus began and ended my political career, although years later living in the United States, I have wondered if I had chosen to remain in England, I might have aspired to become a member of Parliament or some other exalted public servant. That would end up being a road not taken.

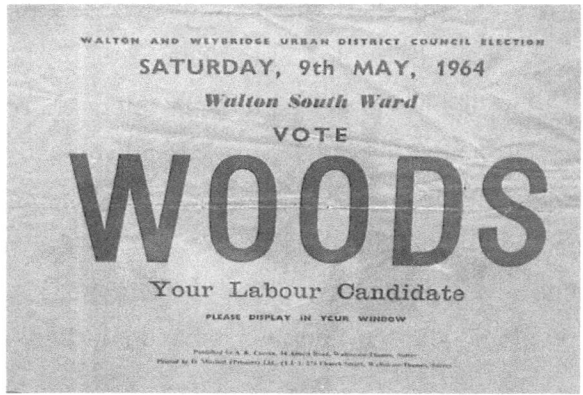

Campaign poster during my run for political office

By this time, the tarnish was off my work in silver. While I had served as a counselor for the various neuroses of the Thames Street inhabitants, I wasn't really getting much counsel myself on what to do next. I had learned somewhere that a definition of material success in life is to understand your abilities—and get paid for them. True, I had infinitesimal journalism experience—but I had taught English for three years, and I did have a bit of a flair for the written word. I decided to take the bold step of emigrating to my father's country, Canada, and to seek opportunities in writing there.

Accordingly, on September 1, 1965, I boarded a Boeing 707 of the British Overseas Airways Corporation bound for Montreal. I wanted to save the world by my writing and wasn't sure where to start. I thought that putting 3,000 miles between me and my future might shed some light on that. A road ahead?

10

O CANADA:
A JOURNALISTIC CAREER AND A FAMILY TRAGEDY

"Why did the Canadian cross the road? To get to the middle."
—Anonymous

I WAS ESPECIALLY EXCITED about traveling to Canada since that was my father's country and I had many relatives there, although I knew them only through wonderful care packages sent to us during the war, containing such remarkable, and for us unattainable, goodies as exotic candies and chewing gum.

As well as the emotional aspect of all this, it was also a year of centenary celebration for Canada's founding in 1867. There was a World's Fair—Expo 67. In several later visits, I sat in on debates in the country's parliament, listening to its prime minister, Lester B. Pearson, a Nobel Prize winner whose name now graces Toronto's International Airport.

It was also a time when Canada was almost ripped apart by Quebec's movement to form a separate state under the premiership of firebrand separatist Rene Leveque. As things turned out, even though at first there was a huge exodus of cars and trucks on route 401, the highway from Montreal to Toronto, the separatist movement has, in the interim, more or less burned out and today it's close to a vestige of its former self.

I had chosen Montreal because of its Frenchness. My cousin Paul who worked in public relations met me there. He drove an MGA sports car and the first day that I stayed with him in his apartment he invited me to drive that low-slung vehicle with the steering wheel on the left through Montreal's rush hour traffic. I was petrified.

Shortly afterwards, I moved into my own apartment in the French speaking part of the city. In short order, I'd been offered a job as a student career counselor at Loyola College (now Concordia University). Why a recruiter would think this was a suitable job for a foreigner just off the plane escaped me. This was a road with potholes!

But I'd happened upon an ad in the Montreal paper seeking an assistant editor for a company called National Business Publications. The company, I discovered, produced such seemingly esoteric periodicals as *Canadian Fisherman*, *Canadian Pulp and Paper*, and *Monetary Times*; but it also boasted one titled *Canadian Doctor.* My resume was thin on the ground, to say the least, so far as editorial experience was concerned, or of medicine for that matter. I applied anyway.

Curious that such a random choice would set the stage for my future lifelong career in medical journalism.

Shortly afterwards, in the doorway to my apartment appeared a rumpled looking character of about 45 with a distinct twitch and with the appearance of a character in one of those newspaper dramas such as *The Front Page*. He announced that he was indeed the editor of *Canadian Doctor* and would grant me an interview then and there since a previously favored candidate had dropped out of contention. Oops, not second-best again! After some perfunctory questioning posed through a haze of cigarette smoke, Bob, as I now knew him to be, offered me the position at $6,000 a year.

Before taking up my position I flew to Halifax to meet my father's sisters. I was greeted there by my Aunt Ethel who, in a reversal of Shakespeare's "Get thee to a nunnery," had in fact leapt over the wall of the convent where she was a nun, following Monica Baldwin's bestseller "I leapt over the wall" and she became a civilian, a teacher of nursing. She met me at the Halifax airport in a fancy car, sporting feminine and distinctly non-nunnish clothing. We drove into the city where Ethel introduced me to her sister Margaret and family, all of them greeting me like a long-lost cousin, which I was.

Ethel showed me around Halifax, pointing out the graveyards of the various Woodses and visiting the family home Pine Haven, located in a sylvan area on the shore of the waters leading to Halifax Harbour, and where their father, my father's father, had committed suicide. It was an emotional visit on several levels, so much so that I collected a beautiful fall maple leaf from the ground and sent it with good intentions to my father in England, a missive that engendered not a word of response. But these were the kinds of setbacks I'd become good at deflecting.

Ethel described the dreadful explosion that occurred in Halifax Harbour in December 1917 in which two ships collided, both carrying tons of explosives. The resulting inferno took 2,000 lives, injured 9,000, and devastated much of the city. Ethel's nursing experience stood her in good stead as she rushed to help the wounded.

So, I set to work on *Canadian Doctor*. The building was a rather dilapidated affair with sloping floors, small windows, and the clanking of printing presses in the basement. National Business Publications, it turned out, was located 20 miles west of Montreal. My apartment was in the tony Notre Dame de Grace section of the city, and within walking distance of the railway station where each day I boarded a steam train that puffed noisily along Montreal's lakeside suburbs, depositing me at Ste Anne de Bellevue, right opposite the publishing company's headquarters. My office had three inhabitants: the editor, a managing editor named Henry, and a secretary who toiled wordlessly through the day and whose first name I never discovered, she being known only as Mrs. Wilson.

My apprenticeship at *Canadian Doctor* was rigorous and demanding. I wrote, I edited, I proofread and, worst of all, I was responsible for the so-called imposition. And an imposition it was. It required poring over a chart showing all the pages of the magazine and placing them in such a way that advertisements in red didn't entangle themselves with those in green. The resulting format then went downstairs to the

French-Canadian printers who set the whole publication in hot type on facsimile pages held together with string. Sometimes, when advertisements came in late it became necessary to undo the whole imposition, sometimes requiring me to be in the office until 10 o'clock at night.

Editor Bob had been a newspaper man with the *Montreal Star*, following which he had a brief career as a television reporter—a role for which he was singularly unsuited given his unprepossessing manner and nervous demeanor, exacerbated by a propensity for heavy drinking. But in the safe harbor of *Canadian Doctor,* he became a hard taskmaster, requiring me to start all my articles with a stellar lead paragraph and to link each paragraph right through the story.

Several of my colleagues were Britons straight off the boat who insisted on driving cars like Austin, MG, and Morris, all of which had considerable difficulty—even refusal—to deal with the bitter Montreal winters. I, on the other hand, had exchanged the rails for the road, and purchased for the princely sum of $1,500 a brand-new Volkswagen Beetle. Thus equipped with a car that invariably started even in freezing weather, I was able to give my colleagues a ride into the city or the inner suburbs, as well as propel myself in the sluggish VW to and from Montreal.

By this time, Georgina Allen, whose relationship with me had ended when she had left for the United States, came to visit me in Montreal. She made several trips from New York City, where she was an *au pair,* and eventually we were married and rented an apartment. Our wedding ceremony was conducted at a Unitarian church with an aunt and three cousins in attendance, and presided over by a preacher who had some weeks earlier officiated at the wedding of Richard Burton and Elizabeth Taylor. Eighteen months later, our son Patrick was born. Our son Andrew was born four years after that.

I toiled as an ink-stained wretch at *Canadian Doctor* for four years—an overture for a lifelong career in medical journalism. I worked there from early 1966 to the end of 1969. Then, as had happened before, a colleague pointed out to me an advertisement for an editor for *Canadian Family Physician*, the official publication of the College of Family Physicians of Canada. I was one of 48 applicants subjected to lengthy psychological appraisal, and I was offered the job, this time as the first choice. Our family moved to Toronto. It made sense to forsake Montreal for Toronto, for even as a Francophile, I felt that trying to perfect my French in the province of Quebec would be akin to someone trying to perfect their English in Glasgow.

Toronto: A Blossoming Career

I had wanted to earn $10,000 a year before I was 30 and that was the salary: I'd achieved it with three months to spare. Another goal was to buy a Ford Mustang, then all the rage, but the dealer had a three-month waiting list so instead I acquired a very sporty Cortina GT, gold with black stripes. Thus began phase two of my 60-year odyssey in medical journalism.

At this juncture we began to notice Patrick's distinct mobility issue. It turned out he was soon diagnosed with Friedreich's Ataxia, a debilitating neurological disease, apparently autosomal recessive, that affects speech and mobility. The disease must be carried in recessive genes of both parents and can be carried from generation to generation without being detected. His prognosis was confirmed at Toronto's Hospital for Sick Children, where a physician blithely stated and with clearly severely challenged empathy, that Patrick would be "in a wheelchair at 15 and would likely die at 19." However, that turned out to be an accurate prognosis and a road to a ruinous family event.

My boss at the college was its estimable Executive Director, Dr. Donald I. Rice, a man of great sartorial and vocal polish, but who was all too frequently the object of what famed Canadian novelist Margaret Atwood called Canada's "Who do you think you are, eh?" Syndrome--a reference to Canadians' aversion to overt flair or accomplishment or style. In fact, in a *British Medical Journal* review of the history of a Canadian organization, I wrote: "Why did the Canadian cross the road? To get to the middle!" The review continued:

> "Scurrilous allegations of Canada's blandness and Canadians' tentativeness abound; but, having lived there for two decades, and for almost half of that time as an employee of the Canadian Medical Association (CMA), I beg to differ. Canada abounds in colour and character and civility—attributes certainly reflected in its national medical association, an organization as old as the country itself.
>
> But you wouldn't know it from this book. Author John Bennett starts out by flubbing the flyleaf

quote from Rudyard Kipling, and it's pretty much all downhill from there."

On my first day at the college, I accompanied the journal's advertising sales manager to his club for a three-martini lunch. Upon our return, I mentioned to Dr. Rice that this seemed like a very agreeable approach to work—a notion, he was quick to point out, which was not college policy.

A day or two after this, I noticed the ad sales guy walking out of the office carrying proofs of the Journal's upcoming issue. I stopped him in his tracks, pointing out that as the editor, surely I should be looking at the final preprint version. Reluctantly, he gave way, and I went through the publication with him, pointing out that if you're going to use photographs, don't publish them in postage stamp size; if you're going to use headlines, make sure they say something and break in the right place. Some lessons learned at *Canadian Doctor*? During my tenure, I wrote some 60 editorials for the Journal as well as serving as a book reviewer for the *Toronto Daily Star* and the *British Medical Journal,* and having several articles published in *Saturday Review* and *Maclean's* magazine.

At the end of my first year, since advertising had increased dramatically, mainly because of modernizing the publication and making it more relevant to readers, I asked my boss if I could hire an assistant. He agreed and wondered whether I would consider hiring a woman, still a revolutionary notion in the then 1960s. I said that I would hire the best person for the job. As it turned out, that person was a woman, who succeeded me as editor when I left—and stayed there for 13 years. This prompted Dr. Rice to seek my advice on publishing and staffing matters throughout my tenure there, and afterwards.

Living close by was another relative, my father's brother Jack, who had retired from a somewhat lowlier career in the Air Force and had been able to acquire a lifelong ambition to own a farm. That farm was some 30 miles South of Ottawa, and had mainly to do with a collection of docile sheep, some of whom would find their way into the busy kitchen of Jack's wife Carol, whereupon they would be greeted by name, such as "for dinner we'll be dining on Alphonse," not a very gastronomically appealing circumstance for a squeamish city boy.

Then came a bit of hubris, which could have derailed my incipient career (a road upended). The esteemed editor of a publication called *Postgraduate Medicine* had resigned to become editorial director of Modern Medicine Publications, then owned by the *New York Times*. I applied for the job. The publisher of *Postgraduate Medicine* flew into Toronto, met me over dinner at the airport Hilton and proceeded to draw on the tablecloth a chart of the McGraw-Hill hierarchy. A week or two later, he informed me that while I had apparently run a close second (again?), the job had gone to someone much more highly qualified. But I then heard from *Modern Medicine*'s new director that one of the publications for which she was newly responsible was *Geriatrics*—and would I like to be that journal's managing editor. So, I resigned from the CFP editorship and agreed to move to Minneapolis to assume—at age 33, no less—the role of managing editor of *Geriatrics*.

Minneapolis: A Road To Ruin?

The editor job in Minneapolis turned out to be a disaster. Since the job had to be filled quickly and I had no visa, I was put up in a hotel and flown back to Toronto every other week. I was one of the director's boys, the other coming from New York to head up the journal *Modern Medicine*. The existing editorial staff did not take kindly to having two senior people parachuted in. Our boss issued scrawled and mainly indecipherable comments on our respective publications from her aerie at the top of the building where she reputedly smoked 100 Kent cigarettes a day; she seldom appeared in person.

In any event, I resigned after six months as did my counterpart from New York; later I learned that some 30 editorial staffers had also quit. Later, the same publisher who had placed me second in the race to be editor of *Postgraduate Medicine*, wrote me: "I was so sorry to learn about your resignation from *Geriatrics*. Does it make sense for us to talk about your going to work (for us) to head up and launch a Canadian version of *Postgraduate Medicine*?" I demurred.

And so, back to Toronto with no clue about what I'd do next. But as luck would have it, the Canadian Medical Association offered to place me on a monthly retainer. And the Ontario Ministry of Health invited me to write a regular column, *Today's Health*, on public healthcare issues. I wrote 280 editorials, articles and reviews for the Canadian Medical Association, including the lead editorial item titled *Publisher's Page*.

Not liking the Toronto houses I could afford, and liking

the ones I could not, I decided to set up my new freelance life in Niagara Falls, 90 miles from Toronto, where housing was roughly two-thirds the price. Thus began five years as a resident of Chippawa, a suburb of Niagara Falls.

Niagara Falls: The Bucolic Life

In many ways, the Niagara Falls suburb, Chippawa, was perfect, especially after the debacle in Minneapolis. There, I wrote my first book, a commissioned history of the College of Family Physicians of Canada. It was called *Strength in Study* for the College's motto *nostrum in studiis robur,* and was built upon interviews with the first 25 presidents of the then 25-year-old organization.

The first of those was the college's inaugural president, Dr. William Victor Johnson, known as Mr. General Practice of Canada, who glorified in the aphorism, "A general practitioner is a doctor who cures the skin and its contents."

I've always joked that only my mother read this book, but a review in the Niagara Falls newspaper noted that "he has taken an anecdotal approach to the subject that has brought it to fruition with such ease of reading." I also wrote for a delightful Esquire-type magazine called *Quest* on such topics as "Vitamins: Why Massive Doses are a Waste of Money and May be Harmful" and produced 170 versions of the *Today's Health* columns which appeared in more than 100 Ontario newspapers.

It was always a thrill to go to some little town and find my column there, which included public health issues such as protecting oneself from the sun or "Summer's Here: Get Out the Insect Repellent." Those columns underpinned my weekly broadcasts on CKFM's popular program, *Hour Toronto,* and covered such issues as the difference between optometrists and ophthalmologists.

Editor holding forth, circa 1979

At the same time, I was able to indulge my passion for thoroughbred horse racing, taking my two young sons Patrick and Andrew to the picturesque Fort Erie racetrack across the Niagara River from Buffalo. They became fans of one of the more unfashionable jockeys there and I, in a departure from my normal medical beat, conducted interviews with Hall of Fame rider Sandy Hawley and with four pioneering women jockeys. Both pieces appeared in *Maclean's* magazine, as did a Q&A interview with philologist Edwin Newman on issues about the use and abuse of the English language.

Edwin Newman, a notable author and commentator, spoke at the American Medical Writers Association meeting when I collared him to set up an interview at NBC. This steely guardian of correct English, a former NBC News commentator, and author of two widely read books on English usage: *Strictly Speaking* and *A Civil Tongue*, told me that "English is becoming a boneless language, a pompous language, a gassy language, all the flavor and the color are being taken from it."

Improving the way the language is spoken is Newman's distinctive crusade:

DW: Don't you think that the weatherman who talks about a 'shower situation' is really trying to inject some life into the language?

NEWMAN: No, I think the weather forecaster who talks about the shower situation is trying to make what he does sound technical. He doesn't want to say showers or rain, he says shower activity. It sounds better.

DW: Do you think there is any danger that the pendulum could swing the other way and we could have a nation of pedants on our hands?

NEWMAN: I would like people to understand that there is a tremendous amount of fun to be had from language. If used correctly even the wisecracks that mangle the language are forgivable—such as "include me out..." A marvelous phrase.

(Edwin Newman, Canadian Medical Association

Journal; October 31, 1977)

During this period, I served as editor for two books: *The Physician and Canadian Law*, and *Drug Education: Current Issues and Future Directions*. My article titled "Not Tonight Dear, I Have a Cephalgia" appeared in an anthology of Canadian journalism. I began a lengthy connection with the Canadian Medical Association, writing more than 100 articles for the *Canadian Medical Association Journal (CMAJ)*, including its regular Publisher's Page which appeared in each issue's lead pages.

The CMAJ launched a tabloid titled *Mediscope,* which was mercifully short-lived, in part because my coeditors and I met regularly for putting practice and imbibing spirituous liquors on the rooftop of Toronto's famed Park Plaza Hotel. More seriously, I was able to fit in some articles for *American Medical News*, for my former employer at *Canadian Doctor*, for the *Financial Post* magazine, and *Canadian Weekend.*

My time in Chippawa was a delightful interlude during which I became fascinated by the Falls themselves and developed a proprietary interest—especially in the way that in winter the spray from those Falls clung to the leafless trees in a delightful Christmassy way. Many friends and acquaintances were physicians, one of whom, an orthopedic surgeon, was on a constant search for people, and therefore potential patients, coming to grief on icy streets.

I only belatedly found out about the War of 1812, the battle of Chippawa, which was fought in our backyard. Crossing the Niagara River in 1814, American forces sought to capture the Niagara peninsula and defeat British troops; the fighting at Chippawa showed that American troops could stand up to British regulars.

But there were dark clouds on the horizon. The worsening condition of my son Patrick's Friedreich's Ataxia prompted me to accept an offer to become Director of Publications for the Canadian Medical Association and say goodbye to Niagara Falls and hello to Ottawa, Canada's capital, and allegedly the second coldest capital after Ulan Bator in Mongolia.

And so, we packed up the house, loaded the four of us and our anesthetized dog Oscar into a station wagon, and headed to Ottawa. Our worldly goods were to follow in a van, and we had already bought a house in the Ottawa suburb of Nepean. Interestingly, in a down market economy for housing, the CMA had agreed to buy our Chippawa house in order to speed our move to Ottawa.

Brrr Ottawa

My ascension to the role of Director of Publications came at the behest of one D. Laurence Wilson, M.D., Dean of Medicine at Queen's University in Kingston Ontario, who was then president of the Association and who had decided that during his one-year term, he would "fix" the journal which was then awash in red ink and staff disaffection.

Upon my arrival, the physician editor resigned, believing that he should have had the job. I was happy to accept his resignation, prima donna and constant agitator for physician preferment that he was. The news editor also resigned, and although I tried to persuade him to change his mind, he decided to quit. So, my first order of business was to hire two senior people. There was no problem finding a journalist for the news section of the journal; attracting a physician to the scientific editorship presented more of a problem. Ultimately, we settled upon a British, Oxford- trained doctor who had done a little writing for the *Lancet*. He turned out to be a disaster and when told that the editors were screaming for his editorial, announced that "the muse had not yet struck." "But the deadline has!" I protested. He lasted less than a full year in the job before being fired.

I then settled in for what was to be a lengthy stint at the CMA. Throughout that time, I had the services of a loyal, discreet and efficient secretary and a competent staff of some 30 souls. The CMA was a model employer. I was well paid, and traveled at Association expense to Monte Carlo, Bermuda, Mexico, Switzerland, Germany, and to most of the Canadian provinces frequently.

During my time in office, I wrote some 200 editorials, articles and reviews. I conducted published interviews, *inter alia*, with Norman Cousins, William F. Buckley, and Malcolm Muggeridge. I also interviewed each of the incoming CMA presidents in their natural habitat.

In my interview with William F. Buckley, conducted, to my surprise, in an extremely ramshackle high floor office in New York, the editor of the *National Review* and syndicated columnist put his feet on a Naugahyde desk and displayed none of his trademark mannerisms such as the languid stare, the flicking tongue, and the arched eyebrow.

DW: Novelist, journalist, philosopher, and educator. Do you see yourself as a renaissance man?

BUCKLEY: I am a journalist who has been graced with singular insights into political truths. I think modesty about political opinions is really unbecoming.

DW: You have said that you qualify spiritually and philosophically as a true conservative but are temperamentally not of the breed. What is that temperament?

BUCKLEY: It is a conservative virtue to proceed much more deliberately than I tend to do; I'm more impulsive than most conservatives are—or that anyone should be.

DW: Do you feel a sense of vindication at having propounded a conservative point of view for many years and now seeing that the US has adopted that point of view?

BUCKLEY: Not really. I've always known I was right and the fact that the majority of the people, however temporarily, agree with me, makes things more agreeable but there is no sense of vindication. If I had had fewer people agreeing with me today than I did 26 years ago when the *National Review* began I would still say that I'm vindicated by the facts and by those values that ought to commend themselves to thinking people.

DW: Should everyone have the right to vote?

BUCKLEY: People should not have the right to vote who are too young or illiterate. Voting is something of a civic sacrament and to take it without any preparation is to defile it.
(William F. Buckley, Canadian Medical Association Journal; January 18, 1982)

In a conversation held on the campus of UCLA with Norman Cousins, the former editor of Saturday Review and a guru of health policy which he taught at the University, he told me the story of his fight with his illness, ankylosing spondylitis, using a combination of massive doses of vitamin C and even heftier amounts of positive thinking.

DW: You have written that love, hope, science, faith and laughter have therapeutic value. Can you expand on that?

NC: I followed a systematic regime of *Candid Camera* classics, Marx Brothers movies, EB and Catherine White's *Subtreasury of American Humor* and Max Eastman's *The Enjoyment of Laughter*. I made the joyous discovery that 10 minutes of genuine belly laughter had an anesthetic effect and found that my astronomic erythrocyte sedimentation rate declined. After an account of my illness appeared in the *New England Journal of Medicine*, I received 3000 letters from physicians—most of them in support. This is evidence of the new respect among doctors for the ideas of nonprofessionals and I was invited to teach a course at UCLA on unconventional approaches to Wellness. *(Norman Cousins, Canadian Medical Association Journal; November 8, 1980)*

Author, journalist and former sage of television—a medium he came to despise—Malcolm Muggeridge has been a member of the British Intelligence Service (MI6), a foreign correspondent in Washington and Moscow, editor of the humor magazine *Punch* and deputy editor of the *London Daily Telegraph*. An atheist turned Catholic, he had an encyclopedic mind and an acerbic—and often mischievous—wit. This interview took place in Muggeridge's modest cottage in Sussex.

I was apprehensive to have landed an interview with a person of such stature, knowledge, and lacerating wit. I walked along a lengthy paved pathway leading to his cottage and there I found him wrapped in a blanket and sitting on a rocking chair—not quite the imposing figure I had anticipated. Among the many topics we discussed was the memory of his longtime friend, George Orwell and his move from atheism to Catholicism:

DW: Orwell was a great hero of yours and I believe you knew him quite well.

MUGGERIDGE: Oh yes, we were friends for many years. He was an extraordinary chap. I think myself that his book *1984* was a bit silly, but *Animal Farm* is a masterpiece and his three or four volumes of collected journalism are brilliant. They stand up today. So lucid.

DW: Was he really a socialist?

MUGGERIDGE: Of a kind. I don't think he was a very strong one.

DW: You've described the institutional church as having crazed clergy, empty churches, and total doctrinal confusion. Do you still perceive it that way?

MUGGERIDGE: I still see a great deal of that. I think that the Catholic Church has many faults but I think it is better than the others.

(Malcolm Muggeridge, Canadian Medical Association Journal; August 15, 1986)

Sometime after our interview, Muggeridge wrote me a kindly letter which I treasure.

Not bad for a callow 30-something heading a 100-year-old, high prestige, international medical publication. And, speaking of international, I undertook an extraordinary series of junkets, writing articles on four major pharmaceutical companies in Switzerland, Germany, Austria, and Britain, and staying first class at hotels such as the Dorchester in London and the Sacher in Vienna.

PARK COTTAGE,
ROBERTSBRIDGE,
SUSSEX.

August 29, 1986.

Mr. David Woods, Editor-in-Chief, CMAJ,

My dear Sir,

May I thank you most warmly
for your presentation of the interview
held in Kitty's and my cottage here in
Robertsbridge, Sussex. I'm used over the
years to being distorted and abused;
you've stuck steadily to what I said
in answer to your questions, and I'm duly
grateful. Many thanks and all good wishes

sincerely,

Malcolm Muggeridge

Personal letter from Malcolm Muggeridge

Tragedy Strikes

From a professional point of view, life was good; from a personal one, it was hell, as Patrick's condition grew steadily worse. Compounding this, the stress became unbearable and affected our marriage, a road leading to filial death and marital strife. First the wheelchair, then the loss of speech and mobility, and finally, in my last year or so at the CMA, his death at 19. Throughout his sickness, the CMA was extraordinary, picking up the tab for a full-time aide.

Patrick was an inspiration not only to us, his family, but to his friends and to his schoolmates, teachers, and health aides he mixed with every day. He left a lasting and profound impression on everyone he encountered. Like many people with serious or debilitating illnesses, Patrick was always upbeat, and always believed that a cure was at hand. He became a fan of Sylvester Stallone and we set up a room full of gym equipment for him in our house where he loved to lift weights and work out.

Andrew, his younger brother, served as an indispensable help to him and as a sort of mini lawyer, and an arbiter in his parents' deteriorating marriage. All of this had a devastating effect on his own health, and he developed ulcerative colitis. I remember taking him to hockey practice on frigid mornings and keeping an eagle eye out for signs of an ataxia that can apparently run in siblings. To compound the unspeakable pain, following Patrick's death and his parents' divorce, his mother was diagnosed with leukemia and died soon afterwards.

Patrick's untimely death occurred after a six-week

stay in the Children's Hospital of Eastern Ontario. He died at 12:30 AM on July the 4th, 1986, and Andrew and I were there saying our goodbyes, including the notation "the great fighter has gone," as noted in my diary. The affection in which Patrick was held was surely demonstrated by the huge turnout at his funeral, including several of his Halifax relatives, Father Michael from the church where Patrick's mother had sung in the choir, and some 30 members of the CMA staff.

Patrick

He was laid to rest near an evergreen tree in Nepean's Pinecrest Cemetery. Two days later, I accepted an invitation to spend a weekend with a friend in Vancouver, but not before

Georgina had sent me a note saying, "I can never forgive you."

Well before that unhappy event, I had long since left the marital home, packing my worldly possessions into the trunk of my Oldsmobile and staying in a succession of motels and hotels before finally renting an apartment within a stone's throw of my CMA office. Andrew came to visit me there on multiple occasions where we'd sit on the balcony and talk endlessly.

As I was writing this, Andrew asked me how I felt at the time of these devastating events. My sense, looking back, is that I tended to compartmentalize to manage the pain. At the same time, though, on multiple occasions each day, I had ventured to the nearby hospital where Patrick was clearly deteriorating. Andrew invented his own form of coping mechanism by traveling the world later on.

Rebounding from his own mentally and physically painful illness and his brother's illness and death, his parents' divorce as well as a few years later, his mother's premature death, Andrew made a decision that would change his life. He set out to explore the world. He landed in the slums of Dublin, Ireland on his own and formed lifelong friendships, meeting scores of characters, and managing a small pub. He later witnessed the IRA riots in Belfast. The crew from Guinness drank in his pub and offered him the opportunity of a lifetime, to manage a pub in Italy. He often tells stories of drinking with Bosnian war criminals who had settled in Italy after the war and hearing the gruesome stories they would tell.

While working in London, Andrew met and married Sarah, his first wife, and moved to her hometown in Wales.

There they had a delightful daughter and named her Cerys, the Welsh for "loved one." Sadly, the marriage lasted only a few years.

Enrolling in an MBA program and fascinated by the rise of China, Andrew befriended classmates from the Middle Kingdom and, after graduating, continued his journey to Shanghai. There he met a Chinese woman, Ying, who had just landed a job in Hong Kong. Deeply in love with this woman, he packed his bags and followed her to Hong Kong.

Andrew and his wife Ying

While teaching at Emlyon, a leading international business school, he had the unique opportunity to teach French students how to navigate the challenges of Chinese business.

He formalized these concepts in a research dissertation, earned a Doctor of Management degree, and authored a popular book, *The Ask*, on how to approach potential clients.

Meanwhile, I had begun to feel that with Patrick's demise plus a messy divorce I was heading towards the top of The Holmes-Rahe Life Stress Inventory in which death of spouse, divorce, marital separation from a mate, and the death of a close family member point to an 80% health breakdown in the following two years. So I needed to separate myself from Ottawa in order to preserve my sanity.

Many roads presented themselves, including one for a teaching position in Halifax, and another a job in communications in Bermuda. The third was a position as VP of publications for a medical publisher in Philadelphia.

11

PHILADELPHIA:
A NEW COUNTRY, A NEW LIFE, AND A NEW WIFE

"America, vot a country!"
–Ukrainian Yacov Smirnoff, comedian

THE EMERGENCY CARE RESEARCH INSTITUTE (ECRI), a Consumer Reports-like organization for medical services, brought me to Philadelphia. ECRI's president was a physician who had never practiced medicine but who wore surgical scrubs because he alleged that the necktie cuts off circulation to the brain and that therefore he was more intelligent than the rest of us. Little did I know that it would be there where a whole new facet of my life was about to unfold.

After two days of interviews with 14 people, I was offered the job (this time, I was the first choice!) and returned to Ottawa to await the special visa that would show that no living

American could possibly hold that job, and which would allow me to work only for ECRI. Weeks went by, and finally I penned a letter to the CEO, saying that in fairness to him and to my 70 putative staff members, I was withdrawing my candidature. But I slept on the letters and the next day the visa showed up. And so, I headed to Philly.

I had visited Philadelphia on two previous occasions, both of which were for meetings of the American Medical Writers Association. Subsequently, I was to serve on the board of directors of that association, and to publish its newsletter. Both times, I had dined at Old Bookbinders famous restaurant. Curious that for some 30 years, I was to have lived within a couple of blocks of that establishment.

In fact, the high spot of my sojourn in Philadelphia was the propitious meeting with the woman who became my darling wife. How did we get together? Well at a time when it wasn't a very fashionable thing to do—and long before the internet, let alone internet dating—I placed a personal ad in *Philadelphia Magazine.* I've said subsequently that it was the best piece of writing I ever penned. It read:

> *"Executive DWM, late 40s, prolific author, presentable, articulate, amusing, seeks dynamic, bright, educated, mannered, whimsical, feminine lady, 33 to 43, for cerebral dalliance initially. Then...?"*

Although blessed with a successful and frenetic professional career, I had not really been afforded many super charged romantic relationships. I determined that I would find someone who had all the qualities listed in my ad and who would also afford me the serenity and tranquility for which I had been searching during most of my recent past.

Shelly

Shelly, it turned out, had all these qualities and many more. We met at a restaurant and started out with a drink at the bar. So far so good. This was followed by dinner, and then by an exploration of the honkytonk South Street and a nightcap at a small bistro near her home. Six weeks into our relationship, we found ourselves in romantic Mexico. One year later on a trip to Wales, I proposed to her in a 13th century Welsh castle and soon after that we were married. Shelly has been my wondrous muse and companion for all these years.

As a doctor's wife and stay-at-home mother, Shelly had little professional experience, but following her divorce, determined to provide for herself, she pulled herself up by her bootstraps, getting an MBA and embarking upon a career in technology at the advent of the personal computer and the internet. Entering the workforce as a single mom in her forties, she climbed the corporate ladder and years later in retirement, kept going when she took on the role of president of the esteemed Cosmopolitan Club of Philadelphia, a private club for professional women like herself.

From the very start, I recognized that Shelly not only had all the attributes listed in my ad, but more than that, she has a lovely voice, a delightful smile, and a wonderful aesthetic. She has been a fabulous companion to me through the various travails of my own mobility and health issues.

And so, we were married. I had moved in with Shelly months before and found myself surrounded by a house full of women—Shelly, her three daughters, even the cat was female! I had no knowledge of or experience with girl offsprings, at least in a paternal sense, particularly since my children were both boys. It was a period of adjustment all around. Over time I have come to develop an increasing bond of affection with my step daughters. I love them dearly.

I was also embraced by Shelly's large extended family. This too was a bit of an adjustment, as we saw her family nearly once a week, and in contrast, I saw my family only once every ten years, whether I needed to or not.

When I joined the family, Jenifer and Melissa were already off the scene in college, but Amanda, at age eleven, was very much a part of the household. Who would have imagined that this Catholic boy would give an address in a synagogue at her bat mitzvah! On a trip to London to introduce Shelly to my parents, Amanda, in typical American fashion, asked my mother where our family was from. "We were always here," my mother replied. Certainly a response that gave short shrift to the Normans, the Romans, and the Vikings!

Shelly and her daughters (L to R): Melissa, Shelly, Jennifer and Amanda

Shelly's parenting imbued the girls with what she called "roots and wings"—providing them a warm home with love and support but letting them fly, and my three stepdaughters have blossomed into accomplished women.

Both older girls, Jennifer and Melissa, are senior executives in their respective fields. Amanda, the free spirit of the family and youngest by many years, was a scholar athlete and, after many years as a serial entrepreneur, is seeking a Master's Degree to support her desire to build a new career in public policy and politics.

Now, after all these years, our girls have presented us with seven beautiful grandchildren. What joy!

Our house, on a little cobbled street in the Society Hill

section of Philadelphia, is a stone's throw from Independence Hall where the Declaration of Independence was signed. It's a four-story affair with plenty of room for all of its denizens, and we lived there for 30 years. We were surrounded by historic Philadelphia, and I often thought that had I been around in 1776, I would surely have been a rebel (a road I might have traveled), dissociating myself from kingly rule. So belatedly, in 1995, I was able to apply for and receive American citizenship.

The culture shock of moving from Canada to the United States was not as great as it might have been since I had always been an admirer of Americans' rugged individualism and market forces—a land of opportunity. Makes one think of the Vicar of Bray from the eponymous 1882 comic opera of the same name who fundamentally changed his principles to remain in ecclesiastical office as external requirements changed around him.

From Corporate VP To High Flying Entrepreneur

My first job at ECRI was to hire a cabinet from among the 70 or so people on my staff. This was composed of five members who met first thing each Monday morning. But first I had to steer clear of some of my colleagues' barbs about the fact that "he's using a typewriter," while they were all using the newfangled personal computers. My embarrassment about this was surely to hide my technological ineptitude which continues to some extent even today, although mitigated by my computer-savvy spouse.

During my five years with the company, I escalated the

revenues from its 30-odd publications by 50%. But as my tenure moved along, I began to perceive that the CEO's megalomania was having an adverse effect upon the publications division. So, while he invested $7 million in an unnecessary addition to the main building, I had to make excuses about why we couldn't pay our printing bills. Finally, early in 1992, the CEO called me into a conference room and announced that since I had accomplished everything that I was hired to do, my position would be ended forthwith.

But I'd anticipated something of the sort and had incorporated a company called Healthcare Media International, Inc. Meanwhile, my first entrepreneurial venture was to start a newsletter on communications for physicians based loosely upon my book, *Paging Doctors*. To my amazement, Jefferson Medical College bought 3,000 subscriptions, and paid for them with an upfront check for $36,000. My eleven-year-old stepdaughter Amanda, described this accomplishment as "really cool."

Emboldened by this, I convinced the director of a large medical malpractice insurance company, persuading him that poor communication is more often a factor in litigation than clinical malfeasance. It took well over a year, but eventually the company agreed to buy 26,000 subscriptions six times a year for six years. This represented a huge boost for my fledgling company. Ultimately, though, the sponsoring company went bankrupt; and so, alas, *Medical Practice Communicator* also fell by the wayside. HMI, though, went on to include among its clients two UK publishing companies, several pharmaceutical firms, and academic institutions.

It's said though that out of darkness cometh light, and that, coupled with my optimism and belief in chance, led to a meeting with Ruth Whittington, a dynamic New Zealander who had founded a medical communications company called Rx Communications. The company was based in a farmhouse near the unfortunately named Welsh town of Mold. She invited me to help develop the company's foothold in the US.

I also started writing for the *British Medical Journal* (BMJ), which published my interviews with FDA Commissioner David Kessler and the head of the trade association representing managed-care insurance companies, Karen Ignani. I went on to write some 20 or so articles and reviews of health policy books for the BMJ, including the much-ballyhooed *Market-driven Healthcare* by Regina Herzlinger, a professor at Harvard.

This led to an invitation from the *Economist Intelligence Unit* (EIU) to write an article on the FDA and another on the information highway in healthcare—a stretch for me since I'm pretty much, as previously noted, technologically challenged. This in turn led to an offer from the EIU to write a book on managed care, whose title was the rather convoluted: *The future of the Managed Care Industry and its International Implications*.

Next came a fun project for Time, Inc., interviewing pharmaceutical executives about the increasing difficulty in getting to see physicians by bribing them with trinkets and junkets. At about this time, as a board member of the International Society for Medical Publication Professionals, I had the honor of serving as editor of that organization's newsletter.

I was very excited to work with Time Inc.'s custom publishing division as moderator of a series of panel discussions involving experts on managed care, ethics, and technology. My book for Oxford-based Radcliffe also had a somewhat unwieldy title: *Communication for Doctors: How to Improve Patient Care While Minimizing Legal Risk.* I also worked with PEPID LLC, a Chicago-based producer of point of care literature. This took me to London and to Los Angeles. Stepping off the plane in London brought back memories of those early years when I was a young whippersnapper in Swinging London. Who would have imagined where this life journey had taken me. Now I could go to the best restaurants and hotels. How far I'd come!

The president of PEPID was a philanthropist and we were invited to attend a gala he sponsored at Mara Lago in Palm Beach. We arrived in our rented Chevy, among Bentleys and Rolls Royces. The ballroom was aglitter, but the event was purely social. This was 2002, long before its current notoriety. Actually, it was a lovely event. And yes, I can personally attest that there *are* chandeliers in the powder rooms.

Academic Recognition And New Roads

Two high points of my career occurred during the first 25 years in Philadelphia. The first was being inducted as a Fellow of the College of Physicians of Philadelphia. As such, we attended dinners, programs, and social events in that historic building and made many acquaintances and friends. I was especially honored, as a non-physician, to be included among so many physician luminaries. I was sponsored at the black tie dinner for new Fellows by Dr. Bob Reinecke, a former president of the Philadelphia Medical Society. The College of Physicians of Philadelphia was founded in 1787 "to advance the science of medicine and thereby lessen human misery." One prominent founding member was Benjamin Rush, one of the signatories of the Declaration of Independence.

The second was particularly rewarding. My alma mater, Magee College, had been absorbed into the University of Ulster, and I was accepted into their PhD program. My thesis supervisor in the US was Dr. Bill Kissick, professor of medicine at the University of Pennsylvania and of health policy at that university's Wharton School. His counterpart in Belfast was Dr. David Baxter, professor of health policy at Ulster University. My thesis was *The Physician of the 21st-Century: Management, Accountability and Information Technology.*

The *viva voce,* or defense of thesis, took place at the Leonard Davis Institute of Health Policy at the university of Pennsylvania's Wharton School and involved three Ulster professors, including Magee's provost and two from North America including Dr. Kissick and Dr. Stuart MacLeod who had been Dean of Medicine at McMaster University in Hamilton, Ontario and a former chairman of my publications committee at the CMA. The first question they posed to me caused me to go blank, but with knees knocking, I managed to prevail. I feared that the planned party for all these people might turn into a wake; but all was well and somebody, much to my surprise and pleasure, called me Dr. Woods. What in the world would my Catholic boarding school teacher Mr. Hobkirk have thought of this!

Later that year, my wife Shelly and I traveled to Belfast and I put on the delightful scarlet doctoral robes of Ulster's Faculty of Health and Social Sciences. It brought to mind hitchhiking through that city 40 years earlier and how far I've come. My family came to the ceremony in Belfast's mammoth convention center, along with hundreds of graduating students and their relatives.

Sitting on a bench with me on the campus of the University of Pennsylvania's Wharton School, are some of my PhD *viva voce* examiners ... and Benjamin Franklin.

So, back in Philadelphia and newly armed with a PhD, I spent five summers teaching a course on medical writing at Jefferson Medical College, truly the opportunity to "give back" whatever I might have learned over many decades of medical communication. Teaching adults, as opposed to snotty kids, required some adjustment, given that the former were much more inclined to challenge my supposed expertise.

And again as a matter of chance, things came pretty

much full circle. My son had died at age 19 of Friedreich's Ataxia at a time when little or no research had been done into that disease. Thankfully, recent research has uncovered a new and encouraging drug against the scourge of Friedreich's. I discovered serendipitously that an organization called the Friedreich's Ataxia Research Alliance was based in Philadelphia. I offered my services and was co-opted on to the organization's communications committee, and invited to write profiles of its researchers and patients. This too was an opportunity to "give back" something as a memorial to my beloved son.

Peace And Serenity At Last

In addition, my own mobility issues became such that living in a four-story house on a narrow cobblestone street became untenable. Living in an area of several prestigious medical centers, I was able to seek diagnoses, but to no avail, and I have learned to live with it. But out of darkness cometh light; we moved to the 36th floor of a gleaming apartment building on Washington Square Park, looking down on Independence Hall, the Delaware River, and the Benjamin Franklin Bridge.

Our view from the 36th floor

I retired my company, and we embarked upon a life of leisure. Keeping a hand in my writing, I started a blog called "The View From the 36th Floor" in which I reflect on wide-ranging topics that take my fancy. Here's a few of the hundred or so I've written:

Socialism: the Apocalypse; or Time to Buy a Volvo?
The National "Elf Service"
Edward Lear: In Praise of Whimsy
Mrs. Malaprop Runs for Precedent
The Age Old Topic of Old Age

I've often heard that those in their golden years say that these are the happiest years of their lives, and for us it's so true. Our neighbors include an eclectic range of delightful people. During the Covid pandemic we called ourselves the Quarantini Group and met for drinks on Zoom on a regular basis. As is often true of folks in their dotage, the meetings always started with a recitation on our various infirmities. We labeled it our "Organ Recital."

And so, taking my cue from the Robert Frost poem, "The Road Not Taken," I've tried to trace my life story along the lines that his poem had a bearing on each stage, and looking at places where I took the road and others where I avoided it. and sometimes where there were potholes or detours. Throughout this exercise I've been guided by the signposts along Frost's travels and his poem served as a remarkable *aide memoire* for the exercise I've tried to undertake.

THE ROAD NOT TAKEN

"I shall be telling this with a sigh
Somewhere ages and ages hence:
Two roads diverged in a wood, and I—
I took the one less traveled by,
And that has made all the difference."

–Robert Frost, American poet

AFTERWORD: PASSIONS

And what if anything have I learned? I'm reliably informed that we come this way but once … so, even in my eighties, it's probably a good thing to have accumulated some convictions and passions. Among these, in the best American traditions, a belief that all people are created equal , and that it's appropriate to treat with respect the people coming down the stairs in the same way you treat the people going up the stairs. Perhaps influenced by my love of thoroughbred horseracing, I've always believed in taking calculated risks. As Rudyard Kipling put it in his poem, *If*:

> *If you can make one heap of all your winnings*
> *And risk it on one turn of pitch-and-toss,*
> *And lose, and start again at your beginnings*
> *And never breathe a word about your loss;*

My Wife

The first and foremost passion, of course, is my dear wife Shelly. She's possessed of all the attributes I looked for in my original advertisement and more. She's a gentle, loving, loyal muse and constant companion. In addition, she's a piano player, knitter, gardener, techie, aesthete, and a fabulously tasteful dresser. Moreover, she reinvented herself in midlife and launched a successful career in technology and business. Throughout our marriage she has looked after our finances, cooked amazing dinners every night, and brought me the serenity and tranquility that I was looking for after the trauma of the Ottawa years.

Grandchildren

I am blessed to have eight of these: Sam, Catherine, Eleanor, Sylvia, Isabel, Dylan, and Maya from my three stepdaughters, and Cerys from my son Andrew and his first wife Sarah. They are a source of joy and inspiration for all of us and represent high hopes for the coming generations.

In-laws

Wilma, Shelly's sister, and Michael Messler. Michael and I went to Monmouth Park races, an expedition designed to check my suitability for marriage to Shelley. The two Messlers have been steadfast friends in the nearly forty years since.

I'm also indebted to my three sons-in-law, Erik, Peter, and Jordan for their continuing love and support.

Thoroughbred Horse Racing

I've been a fan of thoroughbred horse racing since my 20s, and while teaching at a boys' boarding school in England, I was taken by the school's senior master whom we thought was old and wise, but who in fact was a 33-year-old Oxford Balliol classicist, to Epsom Racecourse. It's only in the last few years, having dragged Shelly to 14 racing venues in England, Wales, Canada, Barbados, and the US, that I've been able to achieve what is called "skin in the game." We started with two duds, Another Dilemma and Big Panda, that for all I know are still running, and went on to a pair of contenders: Reine des Lions and Mine for Love, both of which won races.

France

Ever since going to the Lycée de Londres at age six, and three years in Montreal, I've been a lifelong Francophile. I visited France on half a dozen occasions, and have a reasonable knowledge of the French language partly brought about by a *certificat de scolarite* from Philadelphia's Alliance Francaise.

Alcohol and Tobacco

Perhaps I should not classify alcohol and tobacco as passions, but between the ages of 16 and 50, I was a prodigious smoker of cigarettes; at 50, I gave it up cold turkey. And then took up cigars! Expensive cigars! But I gave that up, too, after a few years. In my 20s I drank only beer; then, at 30, I discovered Scotch whisky. Today I enjoy a few drams of The

Famous Grouse every evening along with the now ritual Friday lunchtime martini with various friends.

Politics

More soberly, I've always had a passion for politics. As the saying goes, if you're not a socialist before you're 25, there's something wrong with your heart; if you're not a conservative after 25, there's something wrong with your head.

At the age of 24 when I came to Canada, I supported the leftish new Democratic Party, moved rightwards to the centrist Liberal Party, and finally to the Conservative Party. When I emigrated from Canada to the US, I was very taken with American rugged individualism and market values compared with Canada's more communal values and dirigiste economy. I am now a Democrat, having reacted to the recent tumult in US politics.

As mentioned, I was goaded into running as a Labor Party candidate in UK municipal elections. Besides having "Vote Woods" posters in many windows calling my manifesto "That was the week that was," noted "I do not believe you support the tired old group currently controlling our local affairs; but I do believe that you will want to swell Labor's growing vote on the council ... so vote Labor, vote Woods, vote Saturday May the 9th." In fact ,while I quite predictably lost, I did at least come second among the three candidates.

The Wolves

Watching Wolverhampton Wanderers with my grandson Sam

I've been a fan of the Premier League soccer team the Wolverhampton Wanderers—the Wolves—for 60 or more years, supporting the team through thick and (mainly) thin. That takes passion of a kind. Now, I have infected several of my relatives with strong support of the Wolves. Grandson Sam even on occasion wears the Wolves gold and black colors as we watch their matches together.

Cars

I've always had a passion for cars. My first was a 1935 Ford which was started only by going downhill, or when my prep school students helped by pushing it. Several cars in the UK included two Minis, a Rover 75 whose dashboard looked like an oak tree, and a few cows had died in the making of the hefty leather seats. Add to that a couple more British Fords, a Vauxhall, an Austin, and a Hillman. In North America, I had to learn to drive an automatic, and to drive on the "wrong side of the road." As noted elsewhere, my first car was a VW Beetle. I've owned or leased three Acuras and a Mercedes. My all-time favorite was our most recent car, an Acura TL, which we finally "sold" at 15 years of age and only 50,000 miles to a needy student. We city folk now use Uber or public transport.

Rigorous English Usage

I've long considered myself a guardian of rigorous English usage. For years, I entered the fiendish Polymath crossword in the Financial Times. After all that effort, the Times eventually gave me two prizes: "How to sound really clever" and "So you think you can spell."

The FT Letters pages, noting that its columnist Lucy Kellaway is "a heroine of plain English," also published my enthusiastic support for her, stating, "Lucy bravely sallies forth in vain against 'going forward' and the war against the execrable and ubiquitous 'like' is probably unwinnable, but it may not be too late to turn her guns on two other linguistic villains before they become unstoppable. The first is 'at the end of the day,' which should certainly be terminated well before dusk. The second is 'if you will,' a phrase I heard at least ten times at a recent conference—and which left me decidedly intestate." (From The Financial Times, November 7, 2007, David Woods, PhD, Philadelphia PA.)

INFLUENCES

Several people have influenced my odyssey that I'd like to thank. They include:

My mother—who inculcated in me a love of the English language.

Keith Jones—an early political mentor.

Joe Harvey—a fellow teacher, who introduced me to thoroughbred racing.

Donald Rice, M.D.—who hired me as editor of Canadian Family Physician and became a lifelong friend whom I served as a consultant some six years after.

Woody Freamo—Secretary-General of the Canadian Medical Association and mentor.

Bill Kissick, M.D.—my thesis supervisor and longtime colleague and friend. Bill brought his four Yale degrees to the University of Pennsylvania where he had professorships both at the University and at the Leonard Davis Institute of Health Policy of Wharton School. He and I enjoyed several amiable lunches at the nearby White Dog Cafe talking about my proposed thesis. Just before my dissertation he wrote to me saying that in the many such efforts he had overseen, none had what he kindly described as my level of literacy.

Bob Pendrak, M.D.—who gave a huge circulation boost to Medical Practice Communicator.

Joel Nobel, M.D.—who brought me to Philadelphia and hired me as Vice President Publications of ECRI and then fired me five years later.

Bob Reinecke, M.D.—who launched my 14-year stint as editor and publisher of Philadelphia Medicine and sponsored me for Fellowship in the College of Physicians of Philadelphia.

Shawn Casselberry—co-founder and editor at Story Sanctum Publishing, and a huge help in making this author's work a labor of love.

Michael Birnbaum, M.D.—to whom I'm eternally grateful for ending his marriage to my wife Shelly.

DAVID WOODS BIBLIOGRAPHY

Books

Strength in Study: An Informal History of The College of Family Physicians of Canada, The College of Family Physicians of Canada, 1979, 248 pp

The Future of The Managed Care Industry and Its International Implications, The Economist Intelligence Unit, 1997, 97 pp

Paging Doctors: Messages from a medical journalist, Epigram Publishing, Ottawa, 1984, 179 pp

Communication for Doctors: How to improve patient care and minimize legal risks, Radcliffe Publishing, Oxon, UK, 2004, 125 pp

Assorted articles

For *British Medical Journal*
Texas Medicine
Philadelphia Business Journal
AMA News
American Medical Writers Association Journal
Delaware Medical Journal
Pennsylvania Medicine
Philadelphia Medicine
International Digest of Healthcare Management
Toronto Daily Star
The Philadelphia Inquirer
Quest Magazine

Editorials and Reviews

Canadian Family Physician - 62 editorials

Canadian Medical Association Journal - 280 editorials, articles and reviews

Today's Health – 112 columns

Blogs

WHYY (Public Broadcasting Service):
https://whyy.org/person/david-woods/

Personal website:
https://davidwoods.info/blog

Society Hill Reporter (neighborhood newsletter)

Noteworthy Neighbors (50 items) including an interview with Baruch Blomberg, winner of the 1976 Nobel Prize in Medicine for discovery of the virus that causes hepatitis, and for developing the vaccine that prevents it.